# The Heroine
# or the Horse

# The Heroine or the Horse

## Leading Ladies in Republic's Films

THOMAS BURNETT SWANN

South Brunswick and New York: A. S. Barnes and Company
London: Thomas Yoseloff Ltd

A. S. Barnes and Co., Inc.
Cranbury, New Jersey 08512

Thomas Yoseloff Ltd
Magdalen House
136-148 Tooley Street
London SE1 2TT, England

**Library of Congress Cataloging in Publication Data**

Swann, Thomas Burnett.
  The heroine or the horse.

  Bibliography:  p.
  Includes index.
  1. Republic Pictures Corporation.  2. Moving-
picture actors and actresses—United States—Biography.
I.  Title.
PN1999.R4S95     338.7'61'7914373     76-18483
ISBN 0-498-01962-4

Printed in the United States of America

*To my mother,*

who "walks in beauty, like the night
Of cloudless climes and starry skies;
And all that's best of dark and bright
Meet in her aspect and her eyes."

Lord Byron

# Contents

# In Gratitude . . .

I wish to express a profound indebtedness to the following stars, whose gracious letters have given me information and inspiration for this book:

>Joan Crawford
>John Wayne
>Ann Miller
>Forrest Tucker
>The Late Mari Blanchard

and to

>Adele Mara,

whose letter concerning a different book indirectly suggested to me a history of Republic's leading ladies, and finally to

>Olivia DeHavilland,

who kissed me on the set of *They Died with Their Boots On* (a motherly kiss, I fear; I was almost twelve) and made me unalterably and eternally the devoutest of movie fans.

# Acknowledgments

I am deeply grateful to Maurice Zolotow, whose *Shooting Star* presents John Wayne in both his humanity and his legend; to Gene Fernett, whose Hollywood's *Poverty Row* has supplied me with innumerable facts about Republic and enlarged my respect for the studio; to *Time* magazine, *Newsweek,* and *Variety,* whose movie reviews I have read, sometimes agreeing, sometimes disagreeing, since my boyhood in the forties; to *Whatever Became of. . .?* and *Whatever Became of. . .? (Fifth Series),* which have given me dates, insights, and sympathies; and finally to *Photoplay* and *Silver Screen,* whose pictures and articles introduced me to Republic's leading ladies before I had ever seen them in the theater.

# Picture Credits

The photographs reproduced in this book are courtesy of:

Columbia Pictures
Ann Miller
Paramount Pictures
Republic Pictures
RKO Radio Pictures
Selznick International Pictures
Twentieth-Century Fox Film Corporation
Universal Pictures

# Introduction

Saturday afternoon—school work can wait until Sunday. Magic awaits in the neighborhood movie house (and who can object to popcorn under the seats?). A western with Guinn "Big Boy" Williams tall in the saddle. A horse with flaring nostrils and tossing mane. A quick gun that never misses its target (and never needs reloading). A painted desert and a pretty girl, equally silent, equally meant to be scenic and not interrupt the action. And then, wonder compounding wonder, a twelve-episode serial. Will Red Rider expose the "reputable" banker, Harry Worth, as the leader of rogues who are killing the local ranchers? Can Jim Bowie and Kit Carson save their beleaguered wagon train from landslides and Indian attacks?

Republic is a boyhood memory. Republic is *us* as boys. But unlike Peter Pan, every boy must grow into a man, and growing up is growing out of magic. Why examine a memory? Why not leave it, safe and unalterable, in the enchanted cave of the mind?

Because it is incomplete; because it does an injustice to a small but remarkable studio. Republic, revisited by the man, is incomparably more than serials and Saturday westerns. Thus, this book, affectionate rather than definitive, aimed at the interested layman, not the scholar. Abracadabra! The cave reveals a door. Enter and count the remembered gold. *Add to the trove. . . . The Heroine or the Horse: Leading Ladies in Republic's Films*—my title is incomplete. It is perfectly true that low-budget westerns and serials, often themselves westerns, dominated production in the studio's early days, and that they billed the hero above the heroine and, as often as not, co-starred him with his horse. A typical ad might read:

### GENE AUTRY AND CHAMPION

In

### BLUE MONTANA SKIES

Featuring

Smiley Burnette and June Storey

or

### ROY ROGERS AND TRIGGER

In

### ALONG THE NAVAJO TRAIL

Featuring

George "Gabby" Hayes and Dale Evans

But Republic also made an ambitious western, *Johnny Guitar,* in which Joan Crawford could bust a bronco and outdraw any man, and neither hero nor horse was billed ahead of *her;* and a nineteenth-century musical in which the only duel is fought by piano; and gangster films and supernatural thrillers and campus comedies and every other kind of picture produced by the major studios.

I have chosen a deliberately incomplete title because it will *seem* complete, therefore nostalgic and appealing to those who, seeing them at an impressionable age, remember the early westerns and serials and forget the later and better pictures. Perhaps, thus tempted, they will read my book and discover the full range of Republic's contribution. For the book, whatever its limitation, is much more than a list of heroes and horses and leading ladies who are always led; it is a history of Republic Pictures. Furthermore, it is told through the viewpoint of its actresses.

Ignorance? Inaccuracy? Insanity? Not in the least.

My reason is simple:

Gene Fernett, in one chapter of *Hollywood's Poverty Row,* has expertly told the history with emphasis on the men, and I do not wish to copy him or to risk comparison. I have borrowed from him, it is true, mostly facts, a few conclusions. But my book is not an expansion of his chapter. I have chosen an altogether different approach.

The approach through the actresses seems to me valid because of their large and generally underrated importance to the studio. It is true that John Wayne was Republic's greatest star, and that President Yates engaged, from time to time, such famous actors as Robert Mitchum, Orson Welles, and James Mason. It is also true, however, that he engaged Joan Crawford, Dorothy McGuire, Barbara Stanwyck, Susan Hayward, Maureen O'Hara, Myrna Loy, Ethel Barrymore, Judith Anderson, Ann Miller, Yvonne DeCarlo, and other actresses, lesser of fame but hardly less gifted, and that he had under contract Ann Rutherford, Jennifer Jones, Rita Hayworth, and Carol Landis in the days before they were stars. The ladies who worked for Republic are as countless as the bullets fired in a typical Saturday western. My book is limited to leading ladies, not supporting players, but even they are so numerous that I have had to treat them under separate chapters, or entries within a chapter, to avoid confusion, arranging them chronologically according to the date of the first film they made for Republic; and give them space in proportion either to their *importance to the studio* or the *quality of their work.*

The history of Republic, its rapid rise and its ultimate fall, is largely revealed in its use of its actresses. Such a revelation, far from excluding the men, joins them with the women in their importance to the studio, and, in fact, my most important figure, aside from Yates, man or woman, is John Wayne.

*The Heroine or the Horse* is a tribute to some of the finest actresses and greatest beauties of Hollywood; it is also, I hope, a partial but accurate history of the studio where they worked.

# The Heroine
# or the Horse

# 1 The Man Who Saw Shooting Stars

Herbert Yates liked to make money. At the age of twenty, he went to work for the American Tobacco Company, and, later, Liggett and Myers; by thirty, he had expanded his interests to include oil and become a millionaire. In 1922, he founded Consolidated Film Industries, which processed the films for many studios, just as a printing house may print the books for many publishers. But a laboratory was not a studio; it lacked the potential for growth—and profit. Yates had learned how to work as a small child; he had never learned how to play. He conceived his own studio with the name of "Republic" (after a laboratory he built in World War I); joined with five shoestring companies already in existence, Chesterfield, Invincible, Liberty, Mascot, and Monogram; purchased the old, now vacant, Mack Sennett lot; and announced in 1935 the creation of Republic Pictures. The lot, which had seen pratfalls and pie-throwing in the silent days, was not auspicious. Located in that part of Hollywood variously known as Poverty Row or Gower Gulch, it resembled two adjoining airplane hangars, its adjacent offices merely afterthoughts. Still, it served its modest purpose. For Republic, elaborate sets and large sound stages were not yet necessary. Metro-Goldwyn-Mayer constructed a makeshift town for Andy Hardy and shot a series of pictures without leaving the lot. Republic went to the deserts east of Hollywood for a western; the oil refineries of Los Angeles for a detective drama; Catalina Island or Lake Mono for a South Sea adventure. Later, the Mabel Normand sound stage was added to the lot, and eventually the studio moved its offices to plusher surroundings in North Hollywood. But in 1935, what had served for Sennett also served for Yates.

Three men preceded him as president: W. Ray Johnston, founder of Monogram, who soon withdrew his studio from the complex and resumed independent production;* Nat Levine, former president of Mascot Pictures; and James R. Grainger. But Yates, though fifty-five when Republic was born, was always the power behind the studio, and, though preferring anonymity, soon replaced Grainger as president and became a familiar figure in Hollywood.

In 1935 Republic released its first feature, *Westward Ho*, starring John Wayne, then a little-known B actor, and followed with *Tumbling Tumbleweeds*, starring Gene Autry, who had won a small audience with a radio program and showed to better advantage in movies because he could share the spotlight with his horse, Champion. The following year Yates began to make serials, with men like Ken Maynard, former stunt man and rodeo rider, and Guinn "Big Boy" Williams in the leads, and the company appeared to have settled on inexpensive features and quickly produced serials, with no major stars and no discernible interest in quality or innovation except a strong emphasis on the western.

To the Yates of that period, profit, not art, seemed the all-important word. Even a photograph

*Monogram was absorbed in the fifties by its own subsidiary, Allied Artists, and continues to produce such films as *Cabaret* and *Papillon*.

of the middle-aged founder shows a dour, balding man in a business suit, with the merest hint of a smile that seems to say, "The Dow Jones Average has risen eleven points, but it *might* have risen twenty."

But Yates was more than he seemed to those who worked for his studio, perhaps more than he saw in himself. He was a secret romantic as well as a mundane man of business, and even from the start, Republic fulfilled his dream of the Old West.

Since childhood he had worked hard; while his work with tobacco companies, oil companies, film processing companies had made him more than a millionaire, it was not the sort to encourage escapist dreams. He was a man whose emotional life had been ignored or frozen until his middle years; emotion was nothing to him except the fun of adding dollar to dollar; intellect was everything, and that particular intellectual facet bought, traded, economized in order to multiply: in short, to become rich.

Movie-making was different. Makers of movies have always appealed to the dreams of their audiences. Especially in 1935, when the Great Depression enveloped the country like a gargantuan dust bowl, dreams were in demand. It is not surprising that Yates himself projected a dream into his early films. True, he had the example of other studios before him, and both Columbia and Universal, with which Republic would soon be linked as one of the three "minors" (as compared with the "majors" like Metro-Goldwyn-Mayer and Warner Brothers), made an occasional western and a frequent serial. It was Yates, however, who chose to make Republic the so-called western studio, in serials as well as features: *Flash Gordon* for Universal, *Jungle Menace* for Columbia, *Hawk of the Wilderness* for Republic. Men to ride the horses, women to decorate canyons and mesas.

He presented a Westworld strictly controlled by the law of right over wrong. Its heroes were always heroic; its villains, always villainous; and they bit the bullets their evil deeds deserved. Women? Of course there had to be women, since prepubescent boys were not his only audience (men like himself attended his films). But they were docile and decorative, to say nothing of inarticulate. In other words, a man's man had created a world for men and boys, an escapist world in which the women only existed to serve the men, please them with their looks, and never disturb them with their own needs. Their *raison d'être* was to be captured and rescued, and to give the hero (and those who identified with him) a chance to prove his prowess. Sex? The hero showed more affection for his horse than for his heroine.

Yates, the middle-aged man, began with films for boys—and the boy in himself.

A male chauvinist before the phrase was invented! Of course. But his chauvinism was relatively harmless. Rooted partly in the inexpensive westerns of other studios, which, unlike history, seldom cast their women in central roles, rooted partly in his own experience, it was so naive and well intentioned that neither of those feminist cataloguers of Hollywood history, Molly Haskell *(From Reverence to Rape)* or Marjorie Rosen *(The Popcorn Venus),* took him to task. Republic, unlike our small contemporary studio to which it is sometimes compared, American International, was never an exploitation company. Whatever the public wants, however degrading, American International produces in ghastly supply. Today it is black exploitation: films that pretend to exploit the whites by showing them cold and unscrupulous and deservedly killed by Pam "Foxy Brown" Grier and James "Slaughter" Brown, but that also exploit the blacks by stirring old grievances and present grudges. Today it is crime melodramas that linger on blood-splattered corpses in brilliant Technicolor. Yates did not appeal to the worst in men. He simply shared his dream, limited, yes, but not destructive—a boy's dream of adventure in a simpler time. He did not exploit women, he overlooked them.

Thanks to the shaping force of Yates, who, though sometimes laughably frugal, was never hard and ruthless like Harry Cohn of Columbia, Republic became a place where people liked to work. They worked hard for moderate pay, but enjoyed a camaraderie found in no other studio. Producers, directors, and cameramen took great pride in working with speed and skill on a limited budget. The actors were quick to memorize their lines; willing to play a supporting role in a major production, a major role in a minor production; the model department became the envy of Hollywood. Gene Fernett quotes an early director, Spencer Gordon:

> When we made a production for Republic, we employed players whom we could hire at a low price, but who were the best we could obtain for the money, in order to assure us of peak production for each dollar spent.
>
> Around Hollywood, there is a story about how Republic once sent a film over to Fox to screen, because Republic was proud of the picture and its big sets. The story continues that Fox officials were indeed impressed with the sets, but asked where the actors were—only to be told that Republic started each morning so early that production sometimes began before the actors arrived. . . .

Yates himself personally supervised every movie.

Though he often seemed to strangers a "dour Scotsman," he was really a likable man. He gambled and drank with his actors and crew. He traveled with them to desert or mountain locations and sometimes slept in a tent. Granted, it was hard to talk him into a salary raise—to economize, he replaced the trees and grass around his studio with asphalt and disposed of ten gardeners—but you could joke with him and not get a reprimand or, worse, a swift dismissal; for example, he had placed a cuspidor in every room because he chewed tobacco and liked to spit. A number of actors and actresses moved from bigger studios to Republic, neither for better parts nor better pay, but for happier working conditions. Louis B. Mayer seduced his leading ladies with a promise of better roles. Harry Cohn browbeat the shy Marilyn Monroe, not a singer, into singing her own songs in *Ladies of the Chorus*, among them the delightful but difficult "Every Girl Needs a D-D-Daddy."* Yates was himself seduced by Vera Hruba Ralston, and had he contracted Marilyn for a film, he would have coaxed, instead of browbeaten, her into a song.

Yes, Republic was a good place to work, and women came with the men. Ann Rutherford made three westerns with John Wayne in 1936. Carole Landis and Jennifer Jones (then Phyllis Isley) were under contract to Yates in 1939. In 1940 he signed Judy Canova to a long-term contract, periodically renewed through fifteen years, and he borrowed Claire Trevor, the first of many well-known actresses to co-star with the newly famous Wayne after his hit in *Stagecoach.*

At first he did not know how to recognize a potential star in a young, inexperienced girl. The boy within him suffered growing pains. Carole Landis? Good at stunts, a possible serial queen. Jennifer Jones? Other women were better at riding horses. Vera Hruba Ralston? Foreign, exotic, worldly: in short, a star!* Still, he began to grow (or rather the boy within him), and Republic during the forties and early fifties became inseparable from its leading ladies.

But Yates the businessman and Yates the dreamer did not always live at ease with each other. The man of business shouted, "Economize!" The dreamer shouted, "Experiment!" Though the dreamer grew from boy to youth to man, the growth was often haphazard; the tobacco king, the oil tycoon, was never entirely exorcised. Ironically, in the fifties experiment and not economy was needed to save the studio from that unpredictable giant, television.

Yates experimented—to a point. He borrowed Joan Crawford for *Johnny Guitar;* Maureen O'Hara for *Rio Grande* and *The Quiet Man;* Barbara Stanwyck for *The Maverick Queen.* Almost frantically, it seemed, he was trying to compensate for the minor position women had occupied in his early pictures.** But he was a little too late. The only well-known actress under long-term contract to Yates after 1951 was Judy Canova, and her low-brow humor began to pall as audiences grew in sophistication.

The wonder of Yates was that he was two distinct people in one person; the tragedy was that they differed in age and temperament and were bound to distrust and even dislike each other and never declare a lasting truce.

Republic's leading ladies mirror this conflict and, in effect, Republic.

And now to the ladies.... Who except John Wayne shall introduce them?

*He built her a private skating rink and starred her for sixteen years.

**In 1954, Republic even anticipated the ideal of Women's Liberation with a strong-willed woman (Joan Crawford) dominating a town and, incidentally, her lover (Scott Brady) in *Johnny Guitar.*

*She sang and acted so unprofessionally that Cohn refused to renew her contract. She moved to Twentieth-Century Fox, became a star, and seemed to sing the sizzling "Heat Wave" in *There's No Business Like Show Business,* but her voice was dubbed, if not the sizzle.

# 2 Wayne's Galaxy

Though John Wayne was Republic's one superstar, it was not Yates who made him the most enduring actor in the history of films. He had served an apprenticeship of more than ten years as stunt man, bit player, finally hero of serials and cheap features for Warner Brothers, Twentieth-Century Fox, Paramount, Columbia, Monogram, and Mascot, as well as Republic. At the request of John Ford, United Artists borrowed him from Yates, who had consistently cast him in low-grade pictures, and gave him one of the leads in the classic western, *Stagecoach.*

It is true, however, that Yates, when Wayne returned to Republic after his triumph, starred him in major productions or lent him to other studios to co-star with some of the screen's most distinguished ladies: Paulette Goddard *(Reap the Wild Wind),* Marlene Dietrich *(Seven Sinners and Pittsburg),* Claudette Colbert *(Without Reservations),* Joan Crawford *(Reunion in France.)** Thus, Wayne and Republic continued their association for more than a decade.

Wayne's popularity continued to climb, but even with women like Dietrich and Goddard, he was more convincing a fighter than a lover. In view of this limitation, critics argue the reason for his extraordinarily long and popular career. Does he substitute personal magnetism for acting? Is he an actor so skilled and subtle that he seems to be playing himself when playing a role? The truth appears to lie between the extremes. Rarely more than a competent actor, he learned to isolate those specific aspects of his own personality which were most attractive to his audience, hard-fighting and hard-drinking among them, and present a consistent portrait on the screen: the archetypal pioneer. The portrait is true, but deliberately incomplete. It does not, and does not need to, include sexual charisma; a man who plays action heroes is not expected to be a consummate lover. Though attractive to women on the screen (irresistible to many of his co-stars off screen), he has always made his greatest appeal to men. He has never tried to become a Clark Gable. He is wise. Gable's career, built upon sexual magnetism, had started to falter long before his death, and his title of "King" had become a courtesy, not a right. Even when making *Mogambo* with him in 1953, Grace Kelly complained that she could not fall in love with a middle-aged man whose teeth were false, and fans with long memories sighed for the young Gable of *Red Dust* (1932), the same story with Mary Astor in place of Kelly, and wisecracking Jean Harlow in place of Ava Gardner. Unlike Gable, Wayne has moved easily into character roles* and also managed to remain a star and retain his basic image. He has always seemed more at ease as a friend than a lover to women. In an interview with Jan Goodwin, he says of Maureen O'Hara:

*Maurice Zolotow suggests that Wayne was paired with these ladies because the great romantic idols, Gable, Taylor, and others, had gone to war, while Wayne, because of his age (thirty-four) and a defective shoulder, had been rejected by every service.

*For example, one-eyed Rooster Cogburn in *True Grit* and its sequel with Katharine Hepburn.

18

John Wayne.

Max Terhune, Ray Corrigan, and John Wayne: Republic's
Three Mesquiteers.

She's a great guy—not unfeminine, mind you, far
from it.

But she doesn't mind a little roughhouse if it will
help the film. . . .I've had many friends and I prefer
the company of men. Except for Maureen O'Hara.

Maureen O'Hara a "great guy?" The speaker
could hardly have been Robert Taylor; possibly
Gable, but only with Lombard.

But if not a great lover, an actor can still make
love on the screen; at times, he must. Wayne's early
westerns, the Bs so numerous that his best
biographers have not been able to count them,
include at least a token love affair. In the As the
token becomes significant and perhaps crucial. .
Republic afforded Wayne a variety of actresses,
from the lowliest B to the costliest A.*

*Jennifer Jones and Carole Landis, unknown starlets when
they worked with Wayne, will be considered in later
chapters. So, too, Vera Hruba Ralston, who co-starred
twice with Wayne, and Adele Mara, who appeared in four
Wayne pictures but shared no love scenes with him.

\*     \*     \*     \*     \*

When Wayne was working for Yates in the late
thirties, he was given minor actresses in mannequin
roles, since the audiences who saw his pictures
preferred hard riding to hard loving: Sheila Manors,
Muriel Evans, Phyllis Fraser, Doreen McKay, June
Martel, Pamela Blake—negligible in their day,
forgotten along with their films. Only three of the
B ladies (definitely not B girls—not in an early
western from Republic!) deserve more than a
mention.

Ann Rutherford, who would soon appear in
*Gone With the Wind* and earn a fragile stardom at
Metro-Goldwyn-Mayer as Andy Hardy's sweet-
heart, began her career with Wayne in *The Lawless
Nineties* (1936) and reappeared with him in *The
Oregon Trail* (1936) and *The Lonely Trail* (1936).
Sixteen in her first picture, she gave what Maurice
Zolotow describes as a "sparkling performance,"

John Wayne, Max Terhune, and Ray Corrigan: Republic's
Three Mesquiteers.

John Wayne in *The Rio Grande*.

Max Terhune, John Wayne, and Ray Corrigan: Republic's Three Mesquiteers.

John Wayne with a wounded Richard Jaeckel in *The Sands of Iwo Jima.*

John Wayne and John Agar in *The Sands of Iwo Jima.*

John Wayne in *The Sands of Iwo Jima*.

John Wayne in *Wake of the Red Witch*.

Ann Rutherford.

Ann Rutherford.

Ann Rutherford.

When John Wayne became a star as the young scout in *Stagecoach,* one of his co-stars was Claire Trevor and the scenes he played with her were gentle and moving, thanks in part to John Ford's direction. (Zolotow quotes Ford: "You're stepping on Claire's lines again, kid. Just listen when she talks. Don't rush in.") In *Stagecoach,* Miss Trevor, along with Marlene Dietrich the same year in *Destry Rides Again,* plays the prototype of the blonde whore with the kind heart; such a role was later to become a stereotype *ad nauseum* in westerns beyond number (occasionally revitalized by Marlene herself in *Rancho Notorious* and Stella Stevens in *The Ballad of Cable Hogue*). But Miss Trevor's seeming brass is unalloyed gold. In fact, she was typed in such parts and spent most of her many years in Hollywood somehow managing always to seem the first of her kind.

Before Wayne returned to Republic, RKO reunited him with Miss Trevor in the big-budget *Allegheny Uprising* (1939), a tale that artfully mingles conniving Englishmen, murderous Indians, and gallant settlers in the pre-revolutionary Colonies, with George Sanders, Brian Donlevy, and Chill Wills in support. But it was in *Dark Command* (1940), one of Republic's finest westerns, that he and Claire were most effectively paired. Supported by Walter Pidgeon and Roy Rogers, Wayne and Trevor performed at the peak of their power in this tale of Quantrill's Raiders after the Civil War.

Claire Trevor, though trained on the stage before she entered movies, never attained the heights. After her first three roles with Wayne, she found a secure niche as a character actress, supporting

and the fact that she was engaged for three roles with Wayne in one year testifies to her popularity with the Saturday afternoon crowd. Miss Rutherford, whose movie career declined with her youthful looks—a perpetual ingenue, she could not make the transition of, say, Jennifer Jones or Katharine Hepburn to mature women—emerged from retirement for a cameo in *They Only Kill Their Masters* (1972) with James Garner, but her emergence provoked dismay and not acclaim.

Louise Brooks was an American actress popular in German films such as *Pandora's Box* (1929) and *Diary of a Lost Girl* (1930), but she was totally wasted in *Overland Stage Raiders* (1938), one of Wayne's Three Mesquiteer series, and she retired before the end of the decade. Polly Moran was a vaudeville comedienne who sometimes appeared with Marie Dressler in early sound films and reappeared at the age of fifty-three as the top-billed actress of *Red River Range* (1938). Humorous rather than glamorous, she continued to act in films through *Adam's Rib* (1949), with Spencer Tracy and Katharine Hepburn. But in all of Wayne's early westerns, the horses were more important than the actresses.

It was Claire Trevor who first outstaged the horse.

Claire Trevor, John Wayne, and Walter Pidgeon in *Dark Command.*

25

John Wayne and Claire Trevor in RKO's *Allegheny Uprising*. (Chill Wills to right.)

Wayne as one of the frightened passengers in *The High and the Mighty* (1954) and last appearing in Jack Lemmon's *How To Murder Your Wife* (1965). Her career has been long and distinguished, if somewhat limited in range. She is chiefly remembered for her definitive portrayal in *Stagecoach* and for helping to make a star of her leading man.

### Sigrid Gurie

Sigrid Gurie was one of those foreign imports so beloved by Yates, but her salary demands were slight because, after a big build-up and two major pictures, she had failed to capture the public's affection. Publicity had kept her a well-known name, but insiders knew that, at the age of twenty-nine, she was on the wane. She had starred with Gary Cooper for Samuel Goldwyn in *The Adventures of Marco Polo* (1938), playing the Oriental princess, but audiences had remembered a

John Wayne and Claire Trevor in RKO's *Allegheny Uprising*.

young starlet, Lana Turner by name, and forgotten the dusky Sigrid. She had starred the following year with Charles Boyer in his most familiar film, *Algiers,* but the featured Hedy Lamarr, photographed with unobtrusive brilliance to conceal the inadequacies of her bosom and to hide the fact that her chin was slightly too small for her otherwise perfect features, had captivated the country without even having to act and immediately became an American star. (In Europe she had worked from 1931 and stripped for *Ecstacy* in 1933; the "instant star was a myth.) Nobody noticed Sigrid with Hedy on the scene.

Sigrid's film for Republic, *Three Faces West* (1940), was a long descent from *Algiers,* in spite of John Wayne and a good budget. Furthermore, she complicated production by falling in love with Wayne and pursuing him in such a provocative manner that the off-screen story was far more electric than the film. The on-screen story concerns a Midwestern farmer who leads his friends to Oregon during the dust-bowl days of the Great Depression. Wayne was good in spite of distractions; the story, though a departure from his usual western, was mediocre; and Miss Gurie, miscast, lost her final chance to become an American star. Quickly reduced to low-budget features, she retired from the screen after *Sword of the Avenger* in 1948 and died in 1969.

## Joan Blondell

Plump, saucy, impervious to age, a partridge-in-a-pear-tree sort of a woman, Joan Blondell is a Hollywood institution. She was much in demand for musicals during the thirties—*Footlight Parade* (1933), *Gold Diggers of 1933*— an occasional crime drama like *Bullets or Ballots* with Edward G. Robinson (1936). Never a beauty, she appeared out of place as the glamorous gambling queen accused of murder in Republic's *Lady for a Night* (1941), and Wayne's performance ranged from befuddled to lost. The picture has been forgotten, but Miss Blondell revived her flagging career with her finest film, *A Tree Grows in Brooklyn* (1945), for which she was rumored to win an Academy Award. (Unaccountably, she failed to receive a nomination.)

Most recently, she has published a novel based on her own adventures and starred in a brief television series, "Here Come the Brides." The patina of years becomes both her face and her style, and retirement for such a woman is not in sight.

Joan Blondell.

Joan Blondell.

Joan Blondell.

## Frances Dee

Periwinkle-pretty Frances Dee—prominent in the thirties: Maurice Chevalier's leading lady in *Playboy of Paris* (1931), her first speaking role—starred with Katharine Hepburn in *Little Women* (1933), and Miriam Hopkins in the prestigious *Becky Sharp*, Hollywood's first all-color feature (1935). She was, however, a fading star by 1941, when she appeared with Wayne in *A Man Betrayed*. The picture is notable as a change of pace for him; he plays a lawyer instead of a cowboy and, using wiles as his weapon, he never misses his target, not even the politician who is Frances's father. In spite of its effort at original casting, *A Man Betrayed* remains an indifferent picture, and Frances Dee continued her downward course and, except for the classic horror film *I Walked with a Zombie* and, in the same year, *The Happy Land* (1943), was reduced to featured roles and then retired.

### Ona Munson and Binnie Barnes

Two actresses, though they played the leading feminine roles in Wayne movies, can hardly be designated leading ladies. Rather, they are durable character actresses, like Polly Moran in *Red River Range*, of the sort who often outlast the stars, because they do not depend on their looks. To many, their names remain familiar, and Binnie Barnes, at least, was still at work in 1968, playing a nun with Rosalind Russell and Stella Stevens in *Where Angels Go, Trouble Follows.*

Ona Munson, best remembered as the good-hearted madame in *Gone with the Wind*, appeared with Wayne in *Lady from Louisiana* (1941): Wayne is a young lawyer; Ona's father operates a crooked lottery; hence, the conflict in a lustreless story. Binnie Barnes is a mule-faced, utterly likable female curmudgeon who, with Patsy Kelly, brought a saving humor to the otherwise hackneyed *In Old California* (1942), the saga of a young preacher in the Gold Rush days.* These lively ladies, as unpretentious as they were delightful, played to better advantage with Wayne than those luxuriant but fading stars, Sigrid Gurie and Frances Dee; if they did not offer sensuality, they offered humor, guts, and believability in unbelievable stories, and they seemed at ease with a man whose favorite heroine, Maureen O'Hara, was a buddy as well as a lover.

*Helen Parrish, lesser-billed as Wayne's beloved, had been a successful baby model, then a child actress, but she grew less endearing with each successive phase and never became a star.

Joan Blondell.

John Wayne and Ona Munson in *Lady from Louisiana.*

## Susan Hayward

Susan Hayward, born in a Brooklyn tenement (1918), dreamed of becoming a movie star. She was not, however, a dreamer like Marilyn Monroe, whose climb to fame was assisted first by men, then by pills, alcohol, and analysis, but a tough-minded realist with looks and stamina. First a secretary, then a model, she scorched the cover of the *Saturday Evening Post* and looked so tempting that David Selznick tested her, along with Paulette Goddard, Lana Turner, Bette Davis, and innumerable other actresses, for the role of Scarlett O'Hara in *Gone with the Wind.* The test was a failure* but she stayed in Hollywood and, with the

*Selznick wrote about her: "I think we can forget about Susan Hayward because we don't even need her around as a stand-in for Scarlett...." About Lana Turner: "I think that Turner is completely inadequate, too young to have a grasp of the part, apparently...." Bette Davis, the public's choice, proved unavailable; Paulette Goddard emerged as one of the final four choices, with Jean Arthur, Joan Bennett, and Vivien Leigh.

shrewdness that marked her career at every stage, developed abilities to match her face and reached for the stars. She fumbled through minor roles in major pictures like *Beau Geste* (1939) and major roles in minor pictures like *Our Leading Citizen* (1939); she made her first hit as the pampered socialite in *Adam Had Four Sons* (1941), a role diametrically opposite from her own origins, then was forgotten until Republic cast her as second lead in Judy Canova's *Sis Hopkins* (1941). She left Republic for good but supporting roles at other studios—*Reap the Wild Wind* (1942), *The Forest Rangers* (1942), and *I Married a Witch* (1942), but still the elusive, the ineluctable prize of stardom eluded her. Republic recalled her for *Hit Parade of 1943,* which was not a hit for Susan, but Yates remembered her role with Wayne at Paramount in *Reap the Wild Wind*—she had prettily drowned in a sinking ship—and he cast her as Wayne's co-star in *The Fighting Seabees* (1944). Her competition was formidable. It was a war picture, it was a Wayne picture, and she was intended for the conventional romantic lead. Furthermore, a newly signed starlet, Adele Mara, in the role of Twinkles,

Susan Hayward, starlet.

Susan Hayward, star.

Susan Hayward.

Susan Hayward.

Susan Hayward.

31

**Susan Hayward in *The Saxon Charm*.**

not even billed in the ads, danced so fetching a jitterbug that she was hard to match.* But Susan could not be conventional, whatever the limitations of the script. Her flamboyant looks, more than pretty but less than beautiful, her husky voice, its traces of Brooklyn carefully removed, her salt-and-pepper mannerisms, made her audiences wish for less war and more love, and a more relaxed and believable lover in Wayne.

A recital of later triumphs belongs to history, not Republic: five nominations climaxed by the Academy Award for *I Want To Live* in 1958; her reign with Marilyn Monroe at Twentieth-Century Fox in the lacklustre fifties; her voluntary retirement to become the wife of a Georgia gentleman, Eaton Chalkley, returning rarely to films until his

*Those who watch the picture on television will look in vain for Adele. Her whirlwind dance has yielded to a commercial.

death; her years of anguish and mourning; her reappearance in Hollywood, fires unbanked, with William Holden in *The Revengers* (1972), and her popular television dramas, "Heat of Anger" and "Say Goodbye, Maggie Cole."

In 1973 Susan Hayward was stricken with inoperable brain tumors and given a month to live by her physicians. But Susan, always one to defy predictions, emerged to present an Oscar in the Academy Award ceremonies of April 1974, and revealed a frail but undiminished beauty and an unshaken spirit. In spite of an unbilled streaker and a slim Elizabeth Taylor, she received the biggest ovation of the night.

On March 14, 1975, she died in her Beverly Hills home of a massive seizure. Her physician said, "There was no other case like it; nothing in the medical literature. It was amazing to live that long with this type of lesion. She was one of the great fighters. . . ."

She was also one of the great stars.

Anna Lee in *How Green Was My Valley*.

Anna Lee.

Anna Lee in *Commandos Strike at Dawn*.

## Anna Lee

British-born Anna Lee starred in *King Solomon's Mines* (1937) and other films made in England, but she came to America in 1939 and, a rapidly falling star, appeared as leading lady to Wayne in *The Flying Tigers* (1942). Wayne and another John, an escapee from serials by the name of Carroll, carried most of the action. The dogfights between the Japanese and American pilots were shot with surpassing skill, in spite of the fact that the airplanes came from Republic's model department. But the romantic triangle, involving Wayne, Carroll, and Lee as a nurse, was superfluous and dull. A fallen star by 1944, the game Miss Lee became a supporting player and reappeared with Linda Darnell in *Summer Storm* (1944). In featured roles, she has enjoyed a long and fruitful career, excelling as the happy nun in *The Sound of Music* (1965). She remains a gracious, if too infrequent, presence on television.

## Martha Scott

Martha Scott, trained on the stage, entered movies as the leading lady in *Our Town* with William Holden (1940) and followed with *Cheers for Miss Bishop,* the sentimental but not sentimentalized story of a schoolteacher in a small Midwestern town (1941); then *One Foot in Heaven* (1942), a wise, witty, and wistful picture about a minister and his wife who are both a little unsure of the other foot. She deserved to become a major star. She had the skill and experience. Her face was quietly radiant, if not quite beautiful. Perhaps she was too much the lady. A small-town girl, a schoolteacher, a minister's wife. . .excellent roles, but–*decorous.* After all, Metro-Goldwyn-Mayer had Greer Garson, the lady *par excellence,* and Hollywood, even as with its love goddesses, generally likes only one at a time (after Garson, Grace Kelly). At any rate, in 1943 when she graced Wayne's *In Old Oklahoma,* a story about oil drillers with rugged action (thanks to Wayne) but dull love scenes (thanks to Wayne), she had started her swift decline, and she was quickly reduced to supporting roles in *The Desperate Hours* (1955) and *The Ten Commandments* (1956), and innumerable other films, and later, to frequent guest appearances on television series such as "The Six Million Dollar Man." Her sensitive, mobile face allows her to look harassed or hopeful in every degree of drama or comedy. She has made no attempt to hide her age; her gentle wrinkled face and gray or tinted hair are as gracious as her voice, as graceful as her art.

John Wayne, Albert Dekker, and Martha Scott in *In Old Oklahoma*.

## Ann Dvorak

Ann Dvorak began her career as a dancer in a Hollywood revue, moved to Metro-Goldwyn-Mayer as dancing coach, taught Joan Crawford to kick her heels, and then aspired to stardom in her own right. She won the feminine lead in *Scarface* (1932), and Paul Muni coached her at six every morning to help her refine her performance. Proving herself an actress as well as a dancer, she won a contract with Warner Brothers and made a second hit in *The Crowd Roars* with James Cagney (1932). Success went to her head; worse, to her tongue, and she took to giving interviews with the press in which she accused her bosses of being "slave drivers" and her studio of underpaying her. "Why, a baby in one of my pictures earned more than I did." She snidely concluded, "There are other companies besides Warner Brothers," and sailed for Europe to make pictures in Britain. The pictures were unremarkable, and so were the roles she was offered when she returned to America.

When Yates engaged her for Wayne in *The Flame of the Barbary Coast* (1945), she was thirty-three and no longer hot as a barroom singer to Wayne's cattleman. The role was routine and she walked through most of her scenes. She remained a handsome woman, handsomely photographed, but the featured Adele Mara showed her to disadvantage even in looks.

She continued to act through *The Secret of Convict Lake* (1952), but never fulfilled her promise. Film buffs still conjecture as to why uncommon looks and uncommonly good acting—at least in the early films—did not produce a star. The answer is probably temperament.

## Gail Russell

Ann Dvorak.

Gail Russell was a shy girl whose flawless face led high school friends to describe her to a Paramount executive as the "Hedy Lamarr of Santa Monica." Screentested, she photographed well but acted without distinction. Nevertheless, she was cast in *Henry Aldrich Gets Glamour* (1943) and Ginger Rogers's *Lady in the Dark* (1944), then as the feminine lead to Ray Milland in *The Uninvited* (1944), the story of a girl who is haunted by the ghost of her mother. Eerily photographed, introducing the popular song "Stella by Starlight," the picture showed her to great advantage. She looked so fragile and frightened that the public wanted to protect her, and she was hailed as a star. Long before Marilyn Monroe, vulnerability, no less than sensuality, appealed to the dreamers who are also the moviegoers.

She made four pictures for Republic, interspersed among films for Paramount: *Angel and the Badman* (1947) and *Wake of the Red Witch* (1948) as John Wayne's co-star, *Moonrise* (1948) with Ethel Barrymore, and a melodrama with John Ireland and Mari Blanchard, *No Place To Land* (1958). She lost *Wake of the Red Witch* to the lesser-billed but more animated Adele Mara and *Moonrise* to that notorious stealer of scenes, Miss Barrymore. Nobody, not even the stars, cared to acknowledge *No Place To Land*. But she was adequate as the Quaker girl in *Angel and the Badman*, and she began a friendship with Wayne that led to her being named, perhaps innocently, in a divorce action brought against him by his second wife, Chata. Afterwards, she entered a sanitarium before returning to films.

In two of her pictures for Paramount, *Our Hearts Were Young and Gay* (1944) and *Our Hearts Were Growing Up* (1946), she showed a penchant for humor too rarely tapped, but her otherwise limited gifts, her addiction to alcohol, and her dwindling beauty soon relegated her to low-budget pictures, and in 1961, at the age of thirty-six, she died from a combination of alcoholism and malnutrition. Her body was found in a clutter of whiskey bottles.

She is a tragic example of a beautiful girl promoted to stardom because of her looks, but lacking the talent or will to sustain a career. Hollywood terrified her from the first; terror became her in early films. But dissipation hardened the youthful face, and a desperate woman, unlike a frightened girl, is only appealing if she can act.

Ann Dvorak.

Gail Russell.

Maureen O'Hara.

## Maureen O'Hara

Irish Maureen O'Hara, a great beauty with classic features and natural Titian hair, attended dramatic school and stepped immediately into films. At the age of nineteen she scored in Alfred Hitchcock's *Jamaica Inn* (1939) and followed her first success with a curious combination of minor classics and mediocrities.

She won acclaim for *How Green Was My Valley* (1941), especially for scenes with Roddy McDowell, then an endearing child of twelve. *To the Shores of Tripoli* (1942) and *The Spanish Main* (1945), however, exploited her beauty at the expense of her skill; they were passable imitations of the Errol Flynn movies that drove Olivia DeHavilland to take suspension from Warner Brothers. Stereotyped, so it seemed, in the mediocre by the end of the forties, she returned to the top with John Wayne in two films for Republic, *Rio Grande* (1950) and *The Quiet Man* (1952). In these and three other films she made with him, the pair have come to be associated as closely as Hepburn and Tracy, and the relationship they portray—a strong-willed woman, willingly tamed by a strong-willed man—is one of the most delightful ever portrayed on the screen. *Rio Grande,* directed by John Ford, is chilling with battles between Apaches and settlers; and its love-hate story between a tough cavalry captain and a headstrong Southern belle, ironically his wife, whose home he has burned in the Civil War, is rich with complexities seldom found in a western.

Ford also directed *The Quiet Man,* for which he received an Academy Award. The beauty of Ireland is only surpassed by that of the Irish Miss O'Hara, and conflict flares in a classic fist-fight between Wayne, an American boxer, and Victor McLaglen, the local bully, and again in a rugged courtship, which finds the fiery O'Hara dumped in the mud by Wayne.

Wayne and O'Hara were reunited (though not by Republic) in Ford's *The Wings of Eagles* (1957), *McLintock!* (1963), a hilarious western comedy enlivened by Yvonne DeCarlo*, and *Big Jake* (1971), always to the delight of their fans, and Miss O'Hara has since appeared on a television special with Dick Haymes and the late Betty Grable, singing, dancing, and looking as if she

John Wayne, Maureen O'Hara, and Claude Jarman, Jr., in *The Rio Grande.*

John Wayne and Maureen O'Hara in *The Quiet Man.*

possessed the secret of eternal youth. Recently she announced to the press, "Frankly, I think I am underrated."

Wayne himself is the first to agree:

There's only one woman—other than my three wives—who has been my friend over the years, and by that I mean a real friend, like a man would be.

*Wayne himself secured the role for Yvonne. Her husband had recently lost an eye and almost his life as a stunt man for *How the West Was Won.* Wayne, who played a cameo in the film and knew that Miss DeCarlo was not in demand at the moment, requested United Artists to hire her for his second leading lady.

**John Wayne and Maureen O'Hara in *The Rio Grande*.**

That woman is Maureen O'Hara. She's big, lusty, absolutely marvelous—definitely my kind of woman. . . .

\*          \*          \*

Yates understood and rejoiced that Wayne did not need a woman's help to carry a picture. Ann Rutherford. . . Binnie Barnes. . .Frances Dee. . .Ann. Dvorak. . .Joan Blondell. . .Martha Scott. . .skill, beauty, variety, but no major star with the one exception of Maureen O'Hara, whose career was in a decline when Yates engaged her. (Susan Hayward had only started her climb.) If a story needed a love, and audiences of the forties, even those of Republic, liked at least the implication—why not cast his mistress, Vera Ralston, and let her profit from her co-star's fame? Or borrow descending and inexpensive stars like Sigrid Gurie and Anna Lee, And Dvorak and Frances Dee? Or character actres-

ses like Binnie Barnes and Ona Munsen? The less a lady's fame, the less her fee. Yates, the oil tycoon, had painstakingly learned the movie business, but only to a point. A womanless Wayne was enough to assure a profit. But Wayne with Maureen O'Hara ensured a hit. (If only Yates had borrowed the ladies with whom Wayne worked at other studios . . . Goddard, Colbert, Dietrich, Crawford!)\* One more economy, Yates must have thought at the time when he engaged Miss Gurie instead of, say, Marlene Dietrich. But too many economies equal parsimony.

It was hardly an unforgivable sin for the forties, a prosperous era for films.

But the unjolly giant, television, was not to be felled by a bow and arrow—not in the looming fifties.

\*He did borrow Crawford, but not for Wayne and not until 1954.

# 3 Serial Queens to Stellar Queens

Herbert Yates, a financier of genius, had founded Republic to make millions, not masterpieces. If, at first, he made a considerable fortune, and if he eventually learned a modicum of art from the stars and producers with whom he worked, he nevertheless committed three resounding blunders with actresses under contract to him and hastened, perhaps ensured, the demise of his studio. His first mistake lay in underestimating Carole Landis and Jennifer Jones, whom he featured in two of the ninety-seven serials that Republic and Mascot filmed between 1927 and 1955.

Republic's serial queens, however they titillated the men and boys on a Saturday afternoon, rarely achieved success in feature films. In their own diminutive kingdom, their royalty was as real as their escapability, but studio presidents, mindful of that female audience that ranked romance above action and wept at Bette Davis's "dark victory," attached a stigma to working in serials and treated the queens as mere scullery maids when they aspired to a larger kingdom. Chosen either for helplessness under pursuit or the strength to perform their own demanding stunts—assorted escapes from badmen and beasts—they did not need to act. For Republic, serials and westerns were as closely associated as saddles and horses. Predictable, reliable, repeatable, they helped to support the studio in bolder ventures, the better films for double bills, the costly experiment like *The Spectre of the Rose,* the later John Wayne features, the inevitable failures of Vera Ralston. But serials were an economic necessity, not a source of pride. Who can remember Mala in *Robinson Crusoe of Clipper Island,* a plump, sarong-clad version of Dorothy Lamour?* Phyllis Coates in *Jungle Drums of Africa* and *Panther Girl of the Kongo?* Or even Republic's acknowledged favorite, Linda Stirling, who fled and fought in such economies as *The Tiger Woman* or *Zorro's Black Whip* and is now an English teacher at Glendale College?

In spite of their modest beginnings, several Republic actresses sought a crown of gold instead of brass and achieved minor stardom in feature films. Frances Gifford from *Jungle Girl* (1941) became a respected actress at Metro-Goldwyn-Mayer until her health compelled an early retirement. Spunky Adrian Booth, *The Daughter of Don Q.,* was promoted to modest westerns and starred in *The Gallant Legion* (1948) and *Oh, Susanna* (1953). *Spy Smasher's* Marguerite Chapman (1942) signed with Columbia for a series of thrillers such as *Coroner Creek* (1948) and *Flight to Mars* (1951), and acquitted herself with skill.

Only two actresses, however, climbed from serials to stardom in major pictures.

*With whom she appeared in *Jungle Princess.*

41

**Marguerite Chapman, Republic serial queen.**

## Carole Landis

She was a Roman candle, blazing across the sky, briefly showering sparks, falling into the dark. Like Gail Russell and Marilyn Monroe, she was one of Hollywood's casualties. To the world who saw her films, her lacquered loveliness, she was someone to imitate, never to pity — except for discerning spirits who penetrated the fear behind the eyes, the little girl's face beneath the platinum hair and the carefully pencilled brows. Though she failed to achieve the fame of Marilyn Monroe, she was much the more versatile star, a skilled comedienne, a dramatic actress of growing power, a singer as good as Faye, a dancer as good as Grable. Marilyn seen in person disappointed; Carole might have stepped from the screen.

The public saw her ascent, briefly grieved at the sudden dark, and looked for a newer light. They did not remember that a Roman candle must first be aimed and lit. But Carole, behind the veneer, was honest and unpretentious, and to Gladys Hall (*Photoplay,* December 1941), she told of the backbreaking work before she became a star.

At sixteen she boarded a bus in San Bernadino, California, to make her fame as a singer. She changed her name from Frances Ridste to Carole Landis, and, carrying only the money she had

**Carole Landis.**

**Carole Landis.**

saved as a dime-store clerk, arrived in San Francisco with much ambition and no experience. She waited on tables until she had earned one hundred dollars and headed for Hollywood, where she found a job in a chorus line that Busby Berkeley was training for *Varsity Show* at Warner Brothers. She danced in the film (1937) and several other forgotten pictures, tried a Broadway musical, which promptly failed, and returned, still unknown, to Hollywood.

Warner Brothers cast her as a succession of extras, but Republic gave her a chance—small to be sure, but still a chance—as the leading lady in *Daredevils of the Red Circle,* a gangster serial, not a western, in which she was agile but unrecognizable as a brunette. In the same year, she appeared with John Wayne in *Three Texas Steers,* one of the ubiquitous Three Mesquiteer pictures, and a second western, *Cowboys from Texas* (1939). Her experience almost exactly paralleled that of Jennifer Jones, and the two talented women worked at Republic in the same year. Like Jennifer, Carole was twenty. Wistful and fragile, pretty but not exotic, she failed to impress Yates, who did not renew her contract. It was his misfortune and her good fortune.

The old master, D. W. Griffith of *Intolerance*

**Carole Landis.**

fame, was seeking an unknown actress to star with Victor Mature and assorted dinosaurs in United Artists' *One Million B.C.* (1940). In spite of Carole's own uncertainties, Griffith liked her looks and surmised her gifts. He gave her the part. Those who remember the 1967 Technicolor version, in which Raquel Welch is mercifully silent, cannot imagine the furor created by the original. Not since *King Kong* were dinosaur models constructed with such expense and put to such harrowing use. Scientists argued that man had not been evolved at so distant a time (they have since been proved mistaken), but the public ignored the savants and willingly suspended its disbelief. None of the actors was asked to act, but the musclebound, grunting Mature looked like a caveman, while Carole, far too delicately featured to convince as his girl, was so adorable that, clad in a skin that could hardly have warmed a rabbit, she held her own with Mature and a ravening pterodactyl. Audiences not only forgave her physical unsuitability, they made her an "overnight star" (she who had toiled four years and even gone hungry when she landed in San Francisco with $16.72 in her purse).

But the vulnerables are the victims of fame and love; and, ironically, fame, by placing her in the limelight, made her a victim of opportunists, the men who make use of actresses to advance themselves. Said Carole about her own situation:

> Glamour girls are hard, eh? Glamour girls are self-sufficient, vain, pampered, flattered, foolish, spoiled, too popular to care whether Tom walks out or not because Dick and Harry, twenty of each, are lined up to take his place?
>
> Let me tell you this. . . .The glamour, the tinsel, the fame and the money mean very little if there is a hurt in the heart. . . .So many men in this town want to go out with us, not because they are fascinated, let alone in love, but so they will get their names in the papers the next morning. . . . *Glamour girls are not smart with men. . .*
>
> [Three of her four marriages ended in divorce.]
>
> I want love, marriage, home, children. . . .A sucker? Who? Me?

Still, fame had its compensations, and she followed her hit with a series of modest but well-made pictures like *Mystery Sea Raider* (1940) and *Road Show* (1941), then signed a contract with Twentieth-Century Fox and filmed the expensive thriller, *I Wake Up Screaming* (1941). Reunited with Victor Mature, supporting Betty Grable, she played the murderer's victim, a waitress loved by a cop. The previous year, Miss Grable had excited the public in *Down Argentine Way* with Don Ameche and Carmen Miranda and emerged as a possible threat to Alice Faye as the leading lady of Fox musicals. But she never became a convincing dramatic actress; and Victor Mature had won his tentative stardom by displaying a rugged torso and battling dinosaurs. In *I Wake up Screaming,* he did not get to strip; he lumbered through the scenery or stumbled over his lines. But Miss Landis, foregoing glamour to meet the demands of her role, played the doomed waitress with skill beyond her years and "woke up screaming" fully as well as she had fled from pterodactyls. In *My Gal Sal* (1942), set in the Gay Nineties, she lost Mature to Rita Hayworth (not such a painful loss, perhaps), but she used her experience in chorus lines to rival Hayworth in musical numbers, and the resulting picture, as bright as a Renoir painting come to life, won an Academy Award for Best Art Direction in Color. In 1944 she made a personal triumph of *Four Jills in a Jeep\** with Martha Raye, Kay Francis, and Phil Silvers, a movie disliked by critics, but adored by servicemen for its timely tale of four actresses entertaining the troops. Carole was both relaxed and endearing in helmet and trenchcoat. Next she revealed a comic flair with George Murphy and Pat O'Brian in the light-

*She herself had written the book that inspired the film.

hearted mystery, *Having Wonderful Crime* (1945), which begins with a magic act and ends in murder. *It Shouldn't Happen to a Dog,* with Allyn Joslyn, reaffirmed her as a deft comedienne, and *Thieves' Holiday* (1946), a stylish adventure with George Sanders, allowed her to match her skills with the international actress Signe Hasso. Virginia Mayo was billed ahead of her in the comedy *Out of the Blue* (1947), but lacked her gift for humor and, surprisingly, that of Turhan Bey, straight from the arms of Maria Montez. She seemed to have hit her stride as a wistful clown who could handle drama; often second-billed to another actress, but never second-rate; still at the peak of her looks and improving with each performance.

In many respects she anticipated a contemporary actress, Stella Stevens: both of them gracile blondes, both of them equally at home in drama or comedy and even an occasional musical. In 1949, she appeared, like Miss Stevens, set for a long career as a lesser but multifaceted star. Just as

Stella, entering movies in 1958, has survived such horrors as *Girls, Girls, Girls* with Elvis Presley, *Advance to the Rear* with Glenn Ford, and *Slaughter* with James Brown, to retain her co-starring status and her limited but discriminating audience, so Carole, though few of her films were hits like *One Million B.C.* and *My Gal Sal,* promised to be on hand for many years. Furthermore, she possessed the range for eventual character roles (it may tax the memory, if not the credulity, but Shelley Winters was once a glamorous pin-up). Better pictures, a big promotional push, perhaps could have built her into a major star, but Twentieth-Century Fox had made a box-office queen, first of Alice Faye, then of Betty Grable, and they did not want the expense of another promotion, another blonde. Other studios looked for different "types," for example Madeline Carroll's "lady."

But unlike the stubborn and irreversible Stella Stevens, who plans to produce as well as act, and

Stella Stevens.

Stella Stevens with Ron Howard and Glenn Ford in *The Courtship of Eddie's Father.*

like the less resourceful Marilyn Monroe, Carole Landis succumbed to her vulnerability. In the case of Marilyn, a declining career* and rejection by a lover, variously rumored to have been either Robert or John F. Kennedy, appear to have led to her suicide.

In the case of Carole, career disappointments played little, if any, part. True, she had failed to become a major star, but her last film, *The Silk Noose,* was released after her death and, though modest of budget and filmed in England, testified to continuing demand. But *glamour girls are not smart with men.* The English actor, Rex Harrison, known as Sexy Rexy in his younger days, though married to actress Lili Palmer, engaged Miss Landis in an affair that to him was dalliance, to her devotion. Sexy Rexy, or so he thought, had found the Captain's Paradise—a faithful wife in Miss Palmer, a sometime mistress in the amenable Miss Landis. But Carole did not expect to be sometime; she expected marriage.

It is widely supposed that Rex Harrison ended the affair; it is certain that Carole Landis died from an overdose of sleeping pills.

\*     \*     \*     \*     \*

Because of the parallels in their lives, Carole Landis, to the casual observer, suggests a minor Monroe. But Sydney Skolsky once described her as a "blonde with a difference" (and there were many seductive blondes in her day—Betty Grable, Alice Faye, Virginia Mayo, June Haver, Ilona Massey,

Adele Mara, Adele Jergens). He did not attempt to explain what he meant, but others apparently agreed with him, since Carole Landis has become a legend—not international, it is true—there are no biographies, and there have been no teleplays about her. Still, a legend. Dead, she endures. Wherein lies her difference?

Perhaps it lies in the nature of her affections. Even from the first, Marilyn Monroe used men to advance her career; increasingly she learned to exploit husbands, lovers, and friends. At the start a generous though ambitious girl, she became at the last an ambitious and ungenerous woman. To moralize is both cruel and foolish; her childhood had been a combination of Bedlam and Coney Island. Still, the final result was a woman who did not know how to love. She only lived to be loved.

In contrast, Carole Landis never demanded stardom, acclaim, or love. She offered, and all she asked was to be accepted. At the end, she offered too much. Marilyn asked too much.

*A sucker? Who? Me?*

**Stella Stevens in *How To Save a Marriage—And Ruin Your Life.***

---

*She was thirty-six; Twentieth-Century Fox had recently fired her from *Something's Got to Give.*

Jennifer Jones.

## Jennifer Jones

The only serial actress from any studio to win an Academy Award was Jennifer Jones. Rarely is she associated with serials *or* Republic. A prestige star, she is remembered as David Selznick's discovery, later his wife, and for films produced by Twentieth-Century Fox, Metro-Goldwyn-Mayer, United Artists, and Paramount. But a youthful Jennifer, married to Robert Walker though using her maiden name, Phyllis Isley, filmed a western opposite John Wayne and the serial *Dick Tracy's G-Men* for Republic in 1939.

Maurice Zolotow in *Shooting Star: A Biography of John Wayne,* describes the young Jennifer-Phyllis:

> In one of his [Wayne's] Three Mesquiteers pictures, *New Frontier,* which is concerned with a land-grab scheme to cheat farmers in Texas, [she] was a slender, dark-haired girl of innocent face and luminous black eyes dominating the screen during her few scenes.

Herbert Yates was not impressed. Perhaps she looked too American for a man with a taste in foreign women.* At any rate, after two minor assignments, he allowed her career at Republic to languish and die. But Jennifer and her husband were as determined as they were talented. She approached the powerful producer of *Gone with the Wind,* David Selznick, who was greatly impressed by "the dark-haired girl of innocent face." After their first interview, he confused her name with "Phyllis Thaxter" but wired the story editor in his New York office:

> Regarding Phyllis Thaxter: I think decision on whether or not you should test should depend

*Though she was later to play a Eurasian in *Love Is a Many-Splendored Thing* with little help from a cosmetician.

Jennifer Jones in *Duel in the Sun* (David O. Selznick Productions).

entirely upon whether or not you think she is good bet for future apart from "Claudia"....Is this the big-eyed girl we saw in the office who had two children?...Incidentally, if it is the big-eyed girl, I certainly think she is worth testing no matter when she would be available.

He gave her a series of demanding tests, which confirmed his original impression; in fact, he considered her for *Keys of the Kingdom* as well as *Claudia.* But, "I am seriously worried about Phyllis Walker's confession about her previous contract with Republic. . . . For all we know, she is either on suspension at Republic, or signed something that would prevent her from working for somebody else." His investigations allayed his fears: Yates, who had signed her for six months without an option, had no wish to renew the contract.

Then began the metamorphosis of a Republic serial player into a major star. First, a new, alliterative name, "Jennifer Jones," in the style of Mae Marsh and Greta Garbo and, later, Marilyn Monroe and Stella Stevens. Then, exhaustive training, in spite of the fact that, as a girl, she had traveled with her parents' repertory group, performed juvenile roles, studied at the American Academy of Dramatic Arts in New York, married a fellow student, Robert Walker, and gone to Holly-

wood with him for her stint at Republic. Selznick found her a role in a local play, *Hello Out There,* by William Saroyan, and returned her to New York for further studies. In 1942, he introduced her to the press as his "discovery," an actress new to films, and, having chosen Dorothy McGuire for *Claudia* and sold his rights to *Keys of the Kingdom,* loaned her to Fox for *The Song of Bernadette.* (He also launched her husband into movies, which included *See Here, Private Hargrove* and Alfred Hitchcock's *Strangers on a Train,* but the marriage could not survive conflicting careers, and in 1944 she filed for divorce. Robert Walker died in 1951 at the age of thirty-two.)

As the visionary Bernadette, she won an Academy Award for the best performance of 1943, against such favorites as Greer Garson in *Madame Curie* and Ingrid Bergman, another Selznick player, in *For Whom the Bell Tolls.* By this time, sharp-eyed observers had recognized the "discovery" as a former serial player from Republic, but such a disclosure could no longer hurt her career, and she made a series of hits: *Since You Went Away* with Claudette Colbert and a teenaged Shirley Temple; *Love Letters* with Joseph Cotten, who was to star with her again in *Portrait of Jennie; Cluny Brown,* directed by Ernst Lubitsch; and other pictures of both variety and distinction; at the same time, she won a Gallup Poll as the fastest rising actress in America, and four times the Academy nominated her for another award. Republic's only recognition was to re-release *Dick Tracy's G-Men,* with "Jennifer Jones" written in place of "Phyllis Isley," but she still suffered featured billing after the star, the forgotten Ralph Byrd.

To quote Marjorie Rosen in *Popcorn Venus:*

Selznick's forties' career seemed dedicated to immortalizing her as the Ideal Woman: She was his Ideal Mystic in *The Song of Bernadette* (1943), his Ideal Aging Teen in *Since You Went Away* (1944), Ideal Ageless Beauty in *Portrait of Jennie* (1948), and Ideal Spitfire in *Duel.*

The surest proof of the star whom Jennifer might have become to Republic, if cast in better pictures, even westerns, was *Duel in the Sun,* an epic western with which Selznick hoped to equal his *Gone with the Wind.* Critics groaned and proclaimed the downfall of a great producer, but the public applauded and gave to Selznick his second most profitable picture, and one of the top-grossing films in history. Seen today, *Duel* is a stunning escape from the deadpan—some would say dead—westerns of Clint Eastwood and Charles

Jennifer Jones in *The Wild Heart*.

Bronson. True to Homer and the conventions of an epic, events and people are larger than life, large even for the old, semimythical West, and nothing is so extravagant—and temptatious—as Miss Jones, the rare actress who can dominate a genre in which, with a few exceptions like *Johnny Guitar*, the women support the men. Gregory Peck, new to films and more responsive than in his recent pictures, plays her leading man. Joseph Cotten, Lionel Barrymore, Walter Huston, Charles Bickford, Herbert Marshall, Lillian Gish, and Butterfly McQueen surround the stars with power and authority. But Jennifer Jones, the shy Bernadette, justifies Selznick's faith by becoming a wanton halfbreed girl, who comes to live in the ranch of a wealthy cattleman and sets her sights, literally and figuratively, on his incorrigible son, Peck. Needless to say, she gets her man, but after a duel that gives

the picture its title, she and Peck, wielding pistols, fight to the death on the face of a cliff and die in each other's arms. Feminists such as Molly Haskell in *From Reverence to Rape* have attacked the performance because Miss Jones, though properly aggressive for a liberated woman, seeks to entice her man with wiles as old and feminine as those of Delilah. But the consensus falls with John Kobal in *Gods and Goddesses of the Movies:*

Often the romance in films starring a Barbara Stanwyck, Gloria Grahame or Jennifer Jones, lay in their person. Tragedy seemed to stalk them almost from the moment the credits had finished and an ominous chord in the background score prepared us for their entrance. Because the femme fatale proved to be fatal to herself, it turned her from merely erotic into a romantic image. . . .Some stars became popular as types that are later found to be contrary to their

50

Jennifer Jones.

Jennifer Jones in *The Man in the Gray Flannel Suit.*

to Anna Magnani for *The Rose Tattoo,* but the readers of *Photoplay* consoled her with the coveted Gold Medal for the year's most popular actress. In 1957, she gave the definitive screen portrayal of Elizabeth Barrett in *The Barretts of Wimpole Street.* Contrary to the facts, her Elizabeth was shown to be both beautiful and ambulatory, but such discrepancies, if anything, helped a familiar play, with the limitations imposed by the stage, to become a "moving" picture. Because of the times, however, when poets were thought to be better left to the scholars, the film was not a commercial success. *A Farewell to Arms* in the same year was burdened by a poor script, neither Hemingway nor a satisfactory equivalent, a frequent change in directors, and Hemingway's widely quoted remark that Miss Jones was much too old to play his heroine Catherine (she was thirty-eight; she looked twenty-five). The picture, though a moderate success except with those who remembered the earlier version with Gary Cooper and Helen Hayes, severely damaged the reputation of Selznick as producer and his wife as star; and *Tender Is the Night* in 1961 endured the fate of every Fitzgerald novel adapted for the screen: critical bludgeoning.*

own personality—the shy, private Rita Hayworth and the torrid Gilda Hayworth of her films for one, Ingrid Bergman for another, and Jennifer Jones, who belongs among the screen's great Furies, as well.

The obscure starlet dropped by Republic after a run-of-the-underworld serial and a five-day western had won the public and defied the critics in a picture whose grosses could have bought the whole of Republic.

Eventually Jennifer Jones was to marry Selznick, bear him a daughter, Mary, and neglect her career in favor of being a wife. Complementary geniuses, she the actress, he the producer, they loved each other as artists as well as lovers. Oscar Wilde might have said that marriages made in Hollywood usually end in Hell. But Wildean wit would have failed before so devoted a couple. Appearing infrequently after her marriage, wasted in *We Were Strangers* (1949) with John Garfield and *The Indiscretions of an American Wife* (1954) with Montgomery Clift, Jennifer made a resounding comeback in *Love Is a Many-Splendored Thing* (1955), a potential soap opera, which, thanks to the subtle skill with which she moved from an astringent physician to a passionate lover, won her another Academy nomination. She lost the award

Bill Travers and Jennifer Jones in *The Barretts of Wimpole Street.*

Happily married in spite of career reversals, she retired from the screen until the death of her husband in 1964. She attempted a comeback in the English-made *Idol,* a role that had first been offered to Greer Garson, but the picture was poorly distributed, little reviewed, and Jennifer's portrait of the intriguing but amoral heroine who seduces her son's best friend did not rekindle her fame. Finally, in *Angel, Angel, Down We Go,* a

*The Great Gatsby* suffered a similar fate.

**Jennifer Jones.**

**Jennifer Jones.**

low-budget feature for American International in 1969, which ended the abortive screen career of Christopher Jordan, Sibyl Burton's husband after the famous Richard, she essayed a porno star and endured such lines as, "I made thirty stag films and never faked an orgasm."

But great stars can survive egregious pictures. In 1974, at the invitation of Warner Brothers, she accepted a cameo role in Irwin Allen's fifteen-million-dollar *Towering Inferno,* the most successful of the disaster films of the early seventies, and received a Golden Globe nomination for Best Supporting Actress. As the artist Lisolette, she plays a widow with no pretension to youth but never have years so become a woman, and her "cameo" seemed to command. In such star-clustered—or star-cluttered—pseudoepics, characters usually exist to be drowned, dismembered, asphyxiated, or boiled in oil. Nevertheless, Miss Jones competes with William Holden and a svelte Faye Dunaway, Steve McQueen and Paul Newman, and, together with Fred Astaire, steals the picture, not only from the disaster, but from the top-billed stars. She is like a fairy godmother, rescuing children trapped in a smoke-filled room or reforming the wily Astaire, a salesman of charm—and nonexistent stocks. The film is ingenious with special effects, exciting in every scene, but the waste of talented stars would have horrified David Selznick, who knew how to balance spectacle with humanity. To excite is not to move, and the only moving moments involve Miss Jones and Astaire.

\*     \*     \*     \*     \*

As a young girl and still, Jennifer Jones is a great natural beauty. The maiden Proserpine has become the Earth Mother, Ceres. She is, however, an actress whose versatility has sometimes worked against her. For the women who loved her as Bernadette disliked the halfbreed Pearl. And the men who lusted for Pearl were ill-prepared for a brusque Eurasian doctor who proclaimed that work is more important than love. Unfortunately, it is the actors and actresses always recognizable as themselves—Bette Davis, John Wayne, Gary Cooper—that is to say, the personalities—who appear to achieve the greatest fame in Hollywood. But Jennifer's fame is great, if not the greatest. In skill as well as scope, she is the Vivien Leigh of the American screen.

She has survived Republic by many years. She has survived the general decline of women stars and emerged into a time when Paul Newman is paired with Faye Dunaway instead of Robert Redford. If she chooses another retirement after *The Towering Inferno,* she can either continue her work with handicapped children or devote her time to her husband, Norton Simon, and help him enrich the finest private collection of paintings in the world.

If she chooses to act, roles will be waiting for her, Ceres among the stars.

# 4 The Milky Way

Rita Hayworth, Susan Hayward, Myrna Loy, Joan Crawford, Barbara Stanwyck—today we call them superstars. All of them made at least one picture for Republic. Founded by a man whom today's feminists would call a male chauvinist, Republic nevertheless engaged the services, from time to time, of great beauties and brilliant actresses. In Republic's earlier years, some of these women were unknown starlets, like Jennifer Jones and Carole Landis. In later years, when television threatened to usurp Republic's audience for the low-budget features aimed at double bills, President Yates began to improve his quality and, lacking major stars on his own lot, he had to borrow from other companies or from the stage.

Sometimes he borrowed the stars of the stage for supporting roles in his films. Judith Anderson supported Viola Essen and Ivan Kirov in Ben Hecht's *Spectre of the Rose,* the eerie tale of a young ballet dancer, perhaps also a murderer, who is losing his mind, and of the girl who loves him, to her own despair and eventual death. Ethel Barrymore, crusty, grandmotherly, lightened the sorrow and grimness of *Moonrise,* its stark landscape, its story of murder, flight, and capture. Mercedes McCambridge, the voice of the Devil in *The Exorcist,* bedeviled Joan Crawford in *Johnny Guitar.* Maria Ouspenskaya, tiny in stature, powerful in presence, overshadowed the heroine, Catherine McLeod, in *I've Always Loved You.*

For leading roles, sometimes he borrowed freelancing starlets, soon to be famous, or long-established stars from other studios. The pay was fair and, once Yates had moved his original studio from Gower Gulch to North Hollywood, the operational facilities were clean and modern. It is true that few actresses liked to admit that they had toiled for Republic, which never entirely escaped its early reputation. Still, morale was high among both workers and actors, Yates was willful but not tyrannical, movies decreased in number through the fifties, and, if to work at Republic was thought demeaning, to work for television, except in comedy or a prestige show like "Playhouse Ninety," was the last refuge of the fading star.

Many preferred Yates.

## Rita Hayworth

When Rita Hayworth "hit the saddle" for Republic in 1937, she was not remotely the Love Goddess of the forties. Billed as Rita Cansino, she was chiefly known as a Spanish-descended dancer, inclined to overweight; her low hairline and thick, dark hair gave her unremarkable face an almost simian look. Her acting was rudimentary, and she seemed intended for a career of halfbreeds or ignorant Mexicans or, at best, laconic heroines immeasurably less important than the heroes' horses. Her "lead" in *Hit the Saddle,* filmed in five days, was microscopic, and Yates was hardly to blame for not surmising the thoroughbred who was groomed like a nag.

The shy but ambitious Rita dieted to sublime proportions, raised her hairline with the help of

Rita Hayworth, pin-up queen.

electrolysis, dyed the lustreless black to the strawberry-blonde that afforded the title for one of her first hits, and lengthened the tresses to adorn her shoulders. She exchanged "Cansino" for the American-sounding "Hayworth" and, prodded by the twin tyrannies of her own ambition and that of Harry Cohn, became Columbia's biggest star in the forties.

"Cansino," weight problems, hairline, apprenticeship at Republic (and earlier, Mascot): these were concealed from a public that remembered the Three Musketeers of Dumas, not the Three Mesquiteers of five-day westerns. To moviegoers (at least in the forties) stars descended from Mount Olympus, not the side of a horse, and Rita appropriately played the goddess Terpsichore in *Down to Earth* (1947).

Rita Hayworth.

Rita Hayworth.

Rita Hayworth.

Rita Hayworth.

Rita Hayworth.

The young Ann Miller.

## Ann Miller

Ann Miller is an anatomical marvel. From dusky hair to nimble toes, her legs are half of her length. Perhaps anatomy, together with hard work, helps to account for the fact that she had—and has—the quickest and quite possibly the prettiest dancing legs in the world. Born in 1923, claiming 1919 in order to win jobs denied a child, she entered movies when she was fourteen in *New Faces of 1937.* At fifteen she moved from RKO to Columbia and revealed a comic flair in *You Can't Take It with You* (1938), stealing scenes from James Stewart, Jean Arthur, and Lionel Barrymore. She danced in ten more pictures for Columbia, and, looking available but only with hot pursuit, became a serviceman's favorite in *Reveille with Beverly* (1943), ably supported by Adele Mara. She emerged in *Thrill of Brazil* (1946) as a small-budget Rita Hayworth deserving a higher bracket, a caution to Rita that salary demands and frequent walkouts to wed or divorce did not abet her career (or Columbia's coffers). Who can forget her dancing and singing, "I hear you knocking but you can't come in"? (Who was not tempted to knock?) In 1948 she signed with Metro-Goldwyn-Mayer. A dancing miracle, a clown with looks, sexy enough for sin, sweet enough to wed, she danced with Fred Astaire in *Easter Parade* the following year, and stole *Kiss Me, Kate* from Kathryn Grayson and Howard Keel in 1953. When she faded from movies along with the big musicals, she temporarily retired, but returned in the most expensive commercial ever filmed for television, tapping atop a monumental soup can worthy of Busby Berkeley. The public demanded more than a can for her stage, and she went to Broadway for *Mame,* replacing Angela Lansbury. Her singing had ripened since her movie days, and a whirlwind dance was added to the score. After the close of the show, she helped to redeem the dated television revival of *Dames at Sea* with Ann-Margret. In *That's Entertainment* (1974), a retrospective of Metro-Goldwyn-Mayer musicals, her dancing was represented by scenes from *Hit the Deck* and *Small Town Girl.* Traveling to South America to promote the film, she drew enormous crowds, and on her return to New York, she was invited to star in a modernized version of George Gershwin's *Girl Crazy,* hopefully destined for Broadway after a tour on the road.

RKO, Columbia, Metro-Goldwyn-Mayer, television, Broadway, yes, and little Republic: still in her teens, she made two films for Yates, the forgotten *Hit Parade of 1941* and, the previous

Ann Miller today.

year, the remembered *Melody Ranch.* In her winsome autobiography, *Miller's High Life,* she recalls *Melody Ranch* as a "million dollar musical" and not the typical Gene Autry western. Perhaps she exaggerates the cost of the film. Engaging but modest, it runs a scant sixty minutes, the typical length of a Saturday western. Autry as always is an adequacy, a pleasant smile and a passable voice masquerading as a cowboy. Champion, faultlessly groomed, looks as misplaced as his master on the range.

But Miller gives a million-dollar performance.

## Myrna Loy

Myrna Loy: exotic Eurasian in *The Masque of Fu Manchu* (1932); the bright and outspoken wife of William Powell in the six Thin Man mysteries (1934-46); and the eternally youthful character actress, from *The Best Years of Our Lives* with Frederick March in 1946, through the tipsy passenger in *Airport 1975.* Her beauty if not her acting was singular in her Eurasian period; she and William Powell, along with Tracy and Hepburn,

Gene Autry.

Myrna Loy.

present the two most adult and mutually fulfilling marriages ever shown on the screen; and her third and longest phase is so diversified that further performances may extend but hardly enrich her career.

Among her finest pictures as a character actress is *The Red Pony* (1949), which she filmed for Republic. At forty-five, Miss Loy renounced her Thin Man sophistication to play the wife of a rancher, with Robert Mitchum as ranch hand Billy Buck. While the parents bicker, their lonely son finds escape with his red pony. When the pony dies, the parents are reconciled in their son's grief. Adapted from Steinbeck's novel, the picture steadfastly holds to the book and refuses to hurry its pace; characterization takes precedence over action. The result is a western unique for Republic, rare for Hollywood, and enriching to Myrna Loy.

## Joan Crawford

Joan Crawford was the ultimate star. She survived the hard transition from silents to talkies, when the voice must match the face and exaggeration of gesture must yield to subtlety; she moved with painstaking effort disguised as ease, from flappers, to sophisticates, to career women, to dames, to horror queens. After movie exhibitors labeled her box-office poison in the early forties, she retired from the screen, reshaped her image, and returned to win an Academy Award for *Mildred Pierce* in 1945. Greer Garson, the reigning queen at Metro-Goldwyn-Mayer, where Crawford had once held court, embraced her at the presentation and cried, "Well, none of us should be surprised. After all, my dear, you're a *tradition!*"

It was true. Still, she was not too proud to work

Joan Crawford.

for Republic in *Johnny Guitar.* I wrote to ask her memories of the film and received the following reply from her personal secretary, Vivian Zeiger:

> I read your letter to Miss Crawford on the telephone, and she asked me to tell you, "When an actress does only one film at a studio, there are no memories except the hard work of creating a character. It's not like growing up at a studio like Metro for seventeen years." Miss Crawford wishes you great success and thanks you for thinking of her.

Few of her fans can forget the film, however. In 1954 her career was stable but not exciting. Since *Mildred Pierce,* she had made ten pictures. *Sudden Fear* in 1952 had been a chilling hit for RKO; *Torch Song* in 1953, a return to Metro-Goldwyn-Mayer, had required her to sing, dance, and display her shapely legs; and divided the critics but pleased her public. Still, she wanted a major change. Except for a lesser effort in 1930, *Montana Moon* with Johnny Mack Brown, she had never filmed a talking western. For a woman who launched her career as Lucille le Sueur, the little studio was a challenge, not an embarrassment. Pride had never prevented her from accepting a good role, and when she was offered the script of *Johnny Guitar,*

Joan Crawford in *Johnny Guitar.*

Joan Crawford.

she accepted without hesitation. She must have realized the odds against a picture that, filmed in a new and economical process known as Trucolor, cast the little known Scott Brady as her leading man. But she was a gambler, and she usually won. Indeed, in the film she played the proprietess of a gambling house, and the men on hand, mostly railroad workers, met their match in her. The plot was familiar but the script was lean and literate, and Miss Crawford, strong, resourceful, resilient, was never a stereotype. When Brady summoned the courage to confess his love, who except Crawford could murmur, "What took you so long?" and make a cliché into an avowal of passion? Incidentally, throughout her career she was described as beautiful, versatile, powerful, arresting, but rarely seductive. She was said to compel rather than entice her men. But the Crawford of *Johnny Guitar* is as sensual a woman as ever spun a wheel, and to love her seems worth a fortune in gold or cattle.

Trucolor, a muted process highlighting reds and blues, never succeeded in Hollywood; Technicolor, more expensive but also more natural, drove its cheaper rival into oblivion. Still, like her boots and trousers, it was curiously becoming to Miss Crawford's looks. Scott Brady never became a genuine star. He lost his hair and gained a lot of weight, and sometimes he plays a heavy on television. Nonetheless, he seemed a star with Miss Crawford, a thorough professional, not a stealer of scenes, who inspired her leading men to their best performances. Successful but underrated in its day, its star accused of accepting the role for want of better offers, *Johnny Guitar* has become a minor classic, much like *Beat the Devil* with Humphrey Bogart and Jennifer Jones, and it flickers endlessly on college campuses or in private homes. Not until *Whatever Happened to Baby Jane?* in 1962 did Miss Crawford find so choice a role. Not since *Duel in the Sun* had a woman dominated a western and managed to please the men. Not since *Destry Rides Again* (1939) had she managed to please both the men *and* the women.

Republic had filmed a modest masterpiece.

### Dorothy McGuire

Dorothy McGuire had the misfortune to become a major star in her first film, *Claudia* (1943), and, in spite of important roles in expensive pictures, never again to equal the early success. She did not easily win the role. Jennifer Jones was under

**Dorothy McGuire on the set of *A Tree Grows in Brooklyn*.**

**Dorothy McGuire in *A Tree Grows in Brooklyn*.**

66

**Dorothy McGuire in *A Tree Grows in Brooklyn*.**

contract to Selznick, who wrote to his New York story editor:

> My present feeling is that I want Walker [Jennifer's married name] to do *Claudia* and McGuire to do Nora [in *The Keys of the Kingdom*]....I say to you now that it is my sincere hope that Walker will overnight be a star... if we should cast her as Claudia. I am aware of the girl's shortcomings. I have seen her rehearse, I have seen her perform, I have seen her before audiences... and I know the excitement that she causes in audiences. And her test for *Claudia* knocked everyone out here for a loop.

But Selznick, one of the great producers, wisely accepted advice and selected Dorothy because of her stage experience* and, more important, because of her "pixie kind of personality" and

*She had created the part on Broadway.

"the odd shape and contour of her face." In other words, he came to understand the nature of the character. Unglamorous in an age of glamour, Dorothy played Claudia with pathos and charm, and the public forgave—indeed, approved—her plain but endearing face and her fey mannerisms.

She followed Claudia with such successes as *A Tree Grows in Brooklyn* (1945), *The Spiral Staircase* (1945), *Gentleman's Agreement* (1947), and *Three Coins in the Fountain* (1954); and maturing into a mother instead of a pixie, mothered a brood of children and animals (among them an ostrich) in Walt Disney's *The Swiss Family Robinson* (1960). In her last screen appearance, she played the mother of Christ [*The Greatest Story Ever Told* (1965)].

Surprisingly, her better roles included a thriller for Republic, *Make Haste To Live* (1954). In the

Dorothy McGuire.

same year, Yates had borrowed Crawford for *Johnny Guitar.* He was after the major stars, and he baited Dorothy McGuire with an excellent script. Doubtless he remembered her as the deaf mute threatened with murder in *The Spiral Staircase.* At any rate, she hastened to live because her husband, Stephen McNally, returned from prison to kill her (his second try). She and McNally excelled in a fine production.

Still active and motherly on television, she starred in a 1975 made-for-TV movie, *The Runaways,* as well as in the highly acclaimed *Rich Man, Poor Man.* But the older public remembers *Claudia.*

### Yvonne DeCarlo

Yvonne DeCarlo, Canadian-born but resembling a Moorish princess, may seem misplaced with Hayworth and Hayward, Loy and Crawford. No Academy Awards for her, nor even a nomination. Nevertheless, she has weathered changing trends, moved freely from medium to medium and, when seemingly forgotten, emerged again as a star.

She began her career in 1942 with *This Gun for Hire.* The picture belonged to Alan Ladd, but Yvonne was announced by Paramount for the lead in *Rainbow Island* (1944). She lost the role to

**Yvonne DeCarlo in *Flame of the Islands* (with Kurk Kasnar).**

Dorothy Lamour, who belatedly decided not to doff her sarong, but she entered her photograph in a talent contest and won the lead in Walter Wanger's *Salome, Where She Danced* (1945), a picture as foolish and funny as its title. Yvonne was acclaimed a Universal star, and she played exotics from Calamity Jane to Lola Montez to a mulatto belle sold into slavery and rescued by Clark Gable.

In 1964, too old for temptresses, too young to retire, and badly in need of funds to pay the hospital bills of her husband, a stunt man crippled in filming *How the West Was Won,* she submitted to Universal's makeup department and, submerged in grease paint and putty, emerged as Vampira in "The Munsters," a successful television series (1964-66) and then a movie, *Munster, Go Home.* The gateman who greeted her on her arrival at work, remembering no doubt Salome and Lola, frontier gals and river ladies, wailed a protest one morning, "Miss DeCarlo, what have they done to you?"

For moviegoers, it was not surprising to find her a smooth comedienne; she had proved her flair in *The Captain's Paradise* with Sir Alec Guinness (1953), playing in fact the southern half of his paradise. It has aptly been said of her that, if she has never aspired to greatness in any field, she is better than good at everything she attempts. She can sing, dance, and act both comedy and drama, as well as ride a horse with the speed of Calamity Jane (and belt a Scotch).

In 1971 she reappeared in Stephen Sondheim's hit Broadway musical, *Follies.* She had tried for one of the leads but, failing, accepted a smaller role and found herself with the best song in the show, "I'm Still Here." At forty-nine, she delivered the song with the energy of Ethel Merman and a poignancy drawn from her own indefatigable life. After the play had finished its run, she took to the road in *No, No, Nanette* and other touring musicals and even toured Australia. Now she appears in television dramas, recently playing the mother of Frank Langella in *The Mark of Zorro* (1975), but looking as if she could be his sweetheart.

With such a varied career, and with those exotic features dear to President Yates, she could hardly have missed a sojourn at Republic, in *Flame of the Islands* (1955) and *Magic Fire* (1956). Though modest of budget, they were definitely not minor (not with Yvonne on hand). *Flame of the Islands,* featuring James Arness of later "Gunsmoke" fame, casts her as a nightclub singer in the Bahamas (no Lake Mono for latter-day Republic), and the orchidaceous DeCarlo is the rarest blossom in the

Yvonne DeCarlo in Universal's *Slave Girl*.

rare tropical scenery. *Magic Fire,* a romanticized biography of Wagner, lushly filmed in Europe and beautifully scored, presents her as Wagner's greatest love and raises the question of how he found the time to compose. Both pictures were more fun than art (and *Magic Fire* was hardly factual), but where is the painting, where is the statue to equal DeCarlo's looks? Had there been no Ralston, had Yates been a younger man. . . .

### Barbara Stanwyck

Barbara Stanwyck is one of the great survivors. "I've had to push every gate that ever opened to me," she once remarked, but she never lacked the strength or the will. A nightclub dancer, she entered movies in *The Locked Door* (1929); established herself as a rising star in Frank Capra's *The Bitter Tea of General Yen,* the strange but compelling tale of an American missionary's love for a Chinese warlord (1933); and became a major star in *Stella Dallas* (1937), for which she received an Academy Award nomination, and deserved the award. In the role of the all-sacrificing mother who foregoes even the love of a man for her only daughter, she raises potential soap opera to the level of art and curiously anticipates the achieve-

**Barbara Stanwyck in *Christmas in Connecticut.***

**Barbara Stanwyck.**

ment of Joan Crawford in *Mildred Pierce.*

Her career expanded during the forties. *Double Indemnity* in 1944, directed by Billy Wilder, cast her with Fred MacMurray and Edward G. Robinson in the story of a man who murders his mistress' husband to collect his insurance money. The sacrificial mother became a femme fatale, and few actresses have matched her in lethal allure. She became the hunted instead of the huntress in *Sorry, Wrong Number* (1948); an invalid overhears her husband, Burt Lancaster, making plans for her murder; bedridden, unable to summon help by phone, she awaits the arrival of the hired assassin. Her face is an incarnation of fear. She won another Academy Award nomination and also, incidentally, the reputation for being the best screamer in films.

Though Miss Stanwyck closed the decade with a strong performance in *The Lady Gambles* (1949),* the fifties proved a difficult time for her, in private life as well as on the screen. She and Robert Taylor, her husband since 1939, were divorced in 1952, and consolation did not lie in her films. Most

*The screenplay was written by television's Roy Huggins, producer of James Garner's "The Rockford Files" and husband of Adele Mara.

71

Sterling Hayden and Barbara Stanwyck star in United Artists' *Crime of Passion.*

of the great women stars of her generation were in decline, and the scripts she was offered became increasingly weak. In 1956 she accepted the lead in a minor western from Republic, *The Maverick Queen* (1956). She inherited one of the actors, Scott Brady, who had played with Crawford in 1954's distinguished *Johnny Guitar.* Otherwise, the pictures have little in common. Stanwyck's outlaw, willing to give up crime for the lawman she loves, Barry Sullivan, is a portrait compounded equally of menace and mercy, a queen among the peasants. But script, direction, production are vastly beneath the star.

With good scripts impossible to find, she turned to television, played in a well-reviewed but quickly dropped anthology series, and triumphed as the white-haired matriarch of "The Big Valley." She overshadowed her sons, outacted her guest stars, and endeared herself to a generation of young people who had not been born when she made her first films; she represented to them that rare being, an authority figure with class. The series ran from 1965 to 1968, and its reruns are still in demand for syndication.

John Kobal in *Gods and Goddesses of the Movies* summarizes her achievement:

> Edward Albee's vitriolic, aged but ageless, shrew in *Who's Afraid of Virginia Wolf* is like a compendium of all of Stanwyck's best roles, and by right, she was the only American actress who could have given the role in the film any sense. Here was a woman who still clawed and spat because she once had to, and now, no longer knew how to stop. Without a cause to expend this tragic energy on, she turns it on herself. . . .

Barbara Stanwyck is not, perhaps, a great actress. The power of her personality prevents her from effacing herself into a variety of roles. A winning mixture of the tough and the tender, she is always recognizable behind her mask.

Great beauties and great actresses or both: in a word, stars. New as a movie mogul, Yates allowed them to flee to better pay at bigger studios. . .Rita Hayworth. . .Ann Miller. . .Susan Hayward. In the later days, he borrowed them for one or two pictures and did not try to sign them to long-term contracts. On rare occasions, he gave them choice scripts—*The Red Pony* and *Johnny Guitar*—but these were individual ventures whose stars made many successes for other companies. Vera Ralston continued to reign at Republic and drain her kingdom through its enamored king.

# 5 The Asteroids

Republic, whose major productions, requiring major stars, were rare in the thirties and even the early forties, made frequent use of fading stars or perennial starlets: perhaps its own contract players; perhaps players borrowed from the stage or another studio. Economy-minded except with his mistress, Vera, Yates delighted in bargains: women as well as scripts and locations. Sometimes he found a beauty, sometimes a talent; sometimes an actress not even fit for a serial. When an actress came to Republic, she often felt that, because of the studio's dubious reputation, she must perform at her best; just as often, she walked through her role because, after all, Poverty Row was not Beverly Hills. Yates showed impeccable taste with stars like Joan Crawford and Myrna Loy, who had earned their recognition before Republic was born, but his lesser ladies, his asteroids, reveal a tremendous divergence of skill and looks, from women with star potential to women whose worst mistake was to leave the kitchen and face the camera. Republic, in fact, was a microcosm of Hollywood in general, its best and its worst, and not just the "western company."

## Jane Frazee and Gail Storm

Peter Bogdanovich, the producer, recently remarked that Republic had made the worst musicals in the history of films, and promptly proceeded to launch his own production, one of the worst musicals in the history of films, *At Long Last Love* (1975), in which the macho but non-singing Burt Reynolds and the comely model-turned-actress but nonsinging Cybill Shepherd mouth and gesture a medley of Cole Porter classics. Given a choice between a typical Republic musical, foolish of plot, tolerably acted, and the pretentious *At Long Last Love,* it is easy to choose the Republic musical because the least of its stars could sing. Often trained on radio, they did not expect their songs to be dubbed in moderate-budget pictures; they had to sing for themselves, and Constance Moore in *Atlantic City* was worth a dozen Cybills. Inexpensive musicals were a Hollywood staple in the forties for the lesser studios, and often a singer would circulate freely between Republic and Monogram, Columbia and Universal, and achieve a minor stardom. Two such singers were Jane Frazee and Gail Storm (recalled in *Whatever Became of. . .?, Series Five*).

Jane Frazee possessed the credentials of most Hollywood hopefuls: a slim figure, a fresh, pretty face, and friends back home who told her that she ought to be a star. Fortunately, she could sing. Her voice was sweet, her style was individual, and, after a turn (with her sister) in vaudeville, nightclubs, and radio, she went to Hollywood in 1939 and landed a role in Republic's *Melody Ranch* with Gene Autry and Ann Miller. She signed a contract with Universal but returned to Republic for *Calendar Girl* (1947) with Kenny Baker and *The Gay Ranchero* with Tito Guizar (1948), and a series of westerns with Roy Rogers and Trigger.

Republic's singing westerns, unlike their straight musicals, were the undoing of several actresses; in this one genre, the horse, to say nothing of the hero, continued through 1951 to surpass the lady in billing as well as fame; and Jane soon retired and became a real estate broker in Newport Beach, California. She is often mistaken for Doris Day.

Gail Storm survived some early Republic westerns with Roy Rogers and climbed to top-billing in *Woman of the North Country* (1952) with Rod Cameron, John Agar, and Ruth Hussey. But she found her truest stardom on television in "My Little Margie" (1952-55) and "The Gail Storm Show" (1956-59). Both series were comedies, not musicals, and she managed to clown and somehow look peppermint-ice-cream-luscious in the fashion of Lucille Ball. Two hit records in 1955, "I Hear You Knocking" and "Teen-Age Prayer," and "Dark Moon" in 1957 reminded the public that she was a singer as well as a comic, and that she was also a lesser but unextinguished star. Still in demand for dinner theater productions, she has matured from a pretty girl into a dignified woman, one more testament to the durability of Republic's leading ladies.

## Jane Wyatt

Jane Wyatt recalls the famous lines by John Donne:

> No spring nor summer beauty hath such grace
> As I have seen in one autumnal face.

She supported Ronald Colman in *Lost Horizon* (1937), and audiences liked her youthful grace but remembered Shangri-La, and Colman's mellifluous voice, and intaglio-delicate Margo, agelessly young, aging before their eyes. She was *The Girl from God's Country* for Republic in 1940, but Yates was concentrating on his first major film for his new star, John Wayne *(Dark Command),* and God's Country looked like northern California. For four-teen years she starred in unimportant pictures, including a second film for Republic, *The House by the River* (1950), or supported stars in impor-tant pictures like Cary Grant's *None but the Lonely Heart* (1944), but found her greatest fame as the motherly wife of fatherly Robert Young on television's "Father Knows Best" (1954-60).

Grandmaternal, she reappeared as the human mother of half-Vulcan Spock in one of the most enchanting episodes of that enchanted series, "Star Trek." She stole every scene from her logical, long-eared son, and her years seemed a boon instead of a burden.

## Dale Evans

The Poverty Row studios specialized in singing cowboys. Even John Wayne, suggesting a hoarse crow, sang reluctantly in his early westerns for Monogram. Republic discovered two actors and groomed them for stardom in singing westerns—first Gene Autry with his horse, Champion, then Roy Rogers with his horse, Trigger (actually four Triggers, the last of them stuffed and gracing the Roy Rogers Museum in Apple Valley, California). Both cowboys looking as if they belonged in *Rancho Deluxe* instead of *Rancho Notorious,* they nevertheless made millions for Republic; their fame expanded in rural communities, and Rogers, when his movie career had faded along with the singing western, moved successfully into television.

Rogers, much the more durable of the pair, relied on his leading lady as well as his horse to popularize such films as *Song of Nevada* (1944) and *Bells of Rosarita* (1945)–Dale Evans.* Though Rogers and Trigger were billed above the title, and George "Gabby" Hayes preceded her under the title, and actresses like the "Gypsy Bombshell," Estalita Rodrigues, were sometimes "introduced" or "featured" with prominence, it was usually Dale who gave to formula pictures an individual grace.

Pretty as Wordsworth's violet, at ease in detec-tive dramas as well as westerns, she sang with the sweetness of sleigh-bells in a country rough for wagons. The public was overjoyed when the widowed Rogers married her in 1947 and astonished when, retiring from movies in 1951, she equaled his fame by becoming the author of thirteen popular inspirational books, starting with *Angel on My Shoulder.* Simply written, utterly sincere, the books were inspired by the personal tragedy of losing three of their nine children, and, together with their immaculate image, helped to establish Dale and Roy as prototypes of ideal marriage and parenthood. They still make guest appearances on variety shows, or appear in tasteful commercials, instantly recognizable to the American public, and Roy has filmed his first movie in twenty-three years, *Mackintosh and T.J.*

## Eve Arden

Eve Arden looks as ageless and elegant in the Disney feature *The Strongest Man in the World* (1975) as in her two minor musicals for Republic, *Hit Parade of 1943* with Susan Hayward and *Earl Carroll's Vanities* with Constance Moore (1945).

*She had come to Republic in 1943 for a Zane Grey story, *The Westside Kid,* with Don Barry.

Roy Rogers, Dale Evans, and Trigger.

Constance Moore.

Though she entered movies under the name of Eunice Quedons in *Song of Love* (1929), and, together with Fred Astaire in his first film, supported Crawford, Gable, Franchot Tone, and the Three Stooges in *Dancing Lady* (1933), she remained a supporting player except for Republic; she played the wise-cracking friend of the star in pictures beyond number (in a slight variation, the *mother* of the star, Yvonne DeCarlo, *Song of Scheherazade* (1947). Television, however, has starred her in three series, "Our Miss Brooks" (1952-55), "The Eve Arden Show" (1959), and "The Mothers-in-Law" (1967), and frequent guest appearances. She remains unsurpassed as a glamorous comic whose seeming cynicism conceals a kind heart.

### Constance Moore

Constance Moore was a comely woman and a capable singer. Her limitation was that her even, oval features and her well-modulated voice did not distinguish her from a myriad of other talented but unexceptional actresses who aspired to stardom. She lost her best chance in Paramount's *I Wanted Wings* (1941) with William Holden and Ray Milland. The nominal leading lady, she had the misfortune to appear in Veronica Lake's first major film. Miss Moore was custard pie to Veronica's tangy tart, who seduced Ray Milland, inspired a new coiffure throughout the country, and led the government to urge the female workers in defense plants not to imitate her style—the machines might catch the sensual flow of hair.

Forsaken by Paramount, Miss Moore ensconced herself at Republic and starred in minor musicals and westerns—*Atlantic City* (1944), *Earl Carroll's Vanities* (1945), *In Old Sacramento* (1946)—throughout the forties. Her acting was good, her singing agreeable, and her looks improved with age. But she lacked the first and final requisite for stardom: uniqueness.

### Catherine McLeod

Catherine McLeod is one of those actresses who, even from youth, appear to be meant to support instead of star. Herbert Yates unwisely cast her as the lead in an extravagant color production, *I've Always Loved You* (1946), Frank Borzage's tale of a gifted classical pianist and her teacher caught in a feud of love and professional jealousy and forced to compete in a duel—by piano instead of pistol.

The picture failed with public and critics, who urged that Republic leave such stories to Metro-Goldwyn-Mayer. The duel by piano was both unique and tense, and the acting of Catherine McLeod, her teacher, Philip Dorn, Maria Ouspenskaya, and Adele Mara transcended the inequalities of the script. But much of the dialogue was incredibly mawkish, and Miss McLeod, however well she acted, never magnetized; in a phrase, she starred but did not appear a star, and the magnetic Miss Mara emphasized her lack. It was not enough that she spoke her lines with skill. Nor would her plain but expressive features have proved a limitation if she had coruscated. Today she is sometimes seen in character roles on television; she is never less than superb.

### Lenore Aubert

Disheartened by the failure of his beloved, Vera Ralston, to succeed with the public, but still attracted by foreign beauties, Herbert Yates attempted to make a star of Lenore Aubert, a Yugoslavian actress, who traveled to Hollywood in the late thirties with great expectations. Generally overlooked in *They Got Me Covered* (1942) with Bob Hope and Dorothy Lamour and *Action in Arabia* with George Sanders (1944), she nevertheless caught the eye of Yates, and he cast her in the workmanlike thriller, *The Catman of Paris* (1946). The star was publicized by a large—for Yates—campaign in the fan magazines and her picture played in the better theaters. The nineteenth-century sets and costumes, even in black and white, emphasized the allurements of Miss Aubert—with her thin but exquisite features, she might have been called a Vera Ralston with looks—and the Catman was suitably grim and menacing. But Adele Mara supported the star and, infinitely more responsive in her role, also surpassed her beauty. Henceforth, Lenore was reduced to inexpensive pictures such as *Return of the Whistler* (1948) and *Abbott and Costello Meet the Killer* (1950), purely as an ornament, and faded into the limbo reserved for the legion of European actresses who aspired, solely because of their faces, to repeat the success of Garbo and Dietrich and Bergman.

### Viola Essen

Viola Essen was a young ballerina who had gained attention with a dance pantomime in the unsuccessful Broadway musical *Hollywood Pinafore*. Audiences yawned at the stars, William

**Lenore Aubert confronts *The Catman of Paris*.**

Gaxton and Victor Moore, but admired the grace and agility of the unknown dancer. Yates engaged her to star in one of the most esteemed productions ever filmed at Republic, *Spectre of the Rose* (1946), "a story of dark terror and strange love," produced, written, and directed by Ben Hecht, who, alone or with Charles MacArthur, had written such classic screenplays as *The Front Page, Gunga Din,* and *Wuthering Heights.* Co-starred with Ivan Kirov, according to Republic's publicity department "the most beautiful body on the screen," and supported by Judith Anderson, she promised to become a major star. Republic launched an extensive advertising campaign, with ads in newspapers, screen magazines, *Life, Look, Cue,* and other periodicals, and, lest her co-star Ivan feel slighted, they announced his physical dimensions:

Height—6'2"

Weight—189 pounds
Chest—46-1/2"
Waist—29"
Neck—16"
Biceps—16"
Calf—17"

The picture played in major theaters; critics commended Hecht's versatility as writer-producer-director, and Republic's boldness in financing so offbeat a picture. But Viola Essen, pretty, graceful, talented, a better actress than anyone had a right to expect from a woman trained exclusively in the dance, never made another film in Hollywood, and today both she and "the world's most beautiful man," in spite of his twenty-nine-inch waist, are forgotten names. Why? Box office. Ballet does not create movie stars, not even in Rudolf Nureyev, who has taken a fling at films. The public (and clever publicity) has enthroned an ice-skater, Sonja Henie; a swimmer, Esther Williams; a tap-dancer, Ann Miller; numerous singers, popular or operatic, from Jeanette MacDonald to Grace Moore to Barbra Streisand and Liza Minnelli. But never a ballet star. Even the international dancer, Vera Zorina, cast in the prominent role of Maria in *For Whom the Bell Tolls* opposite Gary Cooper, was replaced by Ingrid Bergman when the picture started production. *Spectre of the Rose* brought esteem but not fortune to Republic; and to its dancers, expectations but not recognition.

Natalie Wood.

Natalie Wood.

## Ruth Warrick

Radio singer Ruth Warrick, acclaimed in her day as a capable character actress, starred for Republic in the inexpensive but unforgettable *Driftwood* (1947). But her limitations were abundantly confirmed when she lost the picture to a little known, nine-year-old child named Natalie Wood, who played an orphan adopted by a young physician after her parents die of a virus spread by squirrels. Allan Dwan, the director, remembers Natalie and not the top-billed star. To Peter Bogdanovich he said: "But what really intrigued me after we got going was the ability of the child we found—little Natalie Wood. She had a real talent for acting, an ability to characterize and interpret, and that was a pleasure. Anyway, it was a nice picture to make, but I don't remember much of it."*

With a few changes, the last sentence could apply to Ruth Warrick: an agreeable woman, a pleasant actress, but who remembers her movie debut in *Citizen Kane* (1941)? Or any role in any later film? Or even her television series, "Father of the Bride" (1961)?

To paraphrase Leo Durocher, nice girls finish last, at least in Hollywood.

*Natalie Wood became a teenaged star in *Rebel Without a Cause* (1955), with James Dean and Sal Mineo. She strengthened her stardom as the tormented young heroine of *Splendor in the Grass* (1961). Voluntarily retired since *Bob and Carol and Ted and Alice* in 1969, she plans a comeback with Michael Caine.

The young Orson Welles.

## Ilona Massey

Ilona Massey, a singer in Hungary, was imported to Metro-Goldwyn-Mayer by Louis B. Mayer as a possible threat to Jeanette MacDonald, the "iron butterfly." With her Nordic-flaxen hair, her high cheekbones and slanted eyes inherited from her Magyar ancestors, she was a beguiling mixture of West and East, and one of the sumptuous beauties of her generation. She sang with the purity of Miss MacDonald, and more than the power, and she scintillated in *Rosalie* (1937) and out-performed its stars, Nelson Eddy and Eleanor Powell. But opposite Eddy in *Balalaika* (1939), she enraged a public that, having tolerated Miss Powell, wanted him instantly reunited with Miss MacDonald, and her promise of stardom was never fulfilled.

**Ilona Massey with Lenore Ulric in *Northwest Outpost*.**

**Ilona Massey: Hungarian chic meets Republic's West in *Northwest Outpost* (with Lenore Ulric).**

Ilona Massey with Lenore Ulric in *Northwest Outpost*.

Her later pictures include the leads in two minor musicals, *New Wine* (1941) and *International Lady* (1941), thankless roles in *The Invisible Agent* (1942) and *Frankenstein Meets the Wolfman* (1943), and two films for Yates. In her middle thirties when she worked at Republic, her career fading but not her looks, she was hired by Yates to star with Nelson Eddy in 1947's *Northwest Outpost* (now that Jeanette, somewhat long in the tooth, was playing character roles). Her looks bewitched, her songs beguiled, but operettas, even by Rudolf Friml, had seen their day in the movies. Yates, however, always impressed with continental exotics, hurried to cast her opposite Rod Cameron in *The Plunderers* (1948). The chic Miss Massey and the lumbering Cameron were impossibly paired—champagne with corn liquor—and Ilona left Republic to join Marilyn Monroe as a foil for the Marx Brothers in *Love Happy* (1949).

As John Kobal writes, "... the ornate Hungarians from Vilma Banky on through Ilona Massey, Miliza Korjus to Zsa Zsa Gabor," were

Nelson Eddy and Ilona Massey in MGM's *Balalaika*.

84

Ilona Massey.

"never quite to be taken seriously but decorative in many films."

Long retired as a Washington socialite, Ilona Massey died in 1974.

### Ruth Hussey

Ruth Hussey, trained on the stage, might have become a star in smart professional roles if Rosalind Russell, whom she resembled in looks as well as manner, had not anticipated her. As it was, she often and ably supported the stars of such remembered productions as *The Women* (1939), *The Philadelphia Story* (1940), *H.M. Pulham Esquire* (1941), and *The Uninvited* (1944). For Republic she supported Vera Ralston in an expensive debacle, *I, Jane Doe* (1948), and Gail Storm in her last film, *Woman of the North Country* (1951);

and finally played a lead in *The Lady Wants Mink* (1953), with Dennis O'Keefe – she is the lady, and to get what she wants, she breeds her own mink.

Her last film was *The Facts of Life* (1960), in which she served as a cool counterpoint to the heated antics of Bob Hope and Lucille Ball.

### Jeanette Nolan

Jeanette Nolan was an accomplished actress on the legitimate stage who starred in one major film but failed to become a star. Orson Welles invited her to play his murderous lady in his unconventional version of *Macbeth* (1948), shot on a typical set for a Republic western. But California proved a wretched alternative to the moors of Scotland, and the characters were directed by Welles to speak in

Old Scots dialect, which was unintelligible except to the cast and which had to be redubbed at considerable cost and to the dismay of economy-minded Yates. Belatedly released, the picture confounded the critics, stunned Shakespearean scholars, and lost the public at large. Welles, the former boy genius, was called the middle-aging bore, and Miss Nolan received such blistering notices that her screen career was reduced to featured roles in films like Audie Murphy's *The Guns of Fort Petticoat* (1957). She found her niche, however, in television. Though she failed in her own series, "Dirty Sallie," because of weak scripts and in spite of spirited acting, she continues to thrive as a featured player of limitless range.

### Joan Leslie

Juvenile actress Joan Leslie, beginning in vaudeville, entering movies with *Camille* (1936) at the age of eleven, captivated the public with her natural charm and impressed the Warner Brothers with seeming star potential. They cast her with Humphrey Bogart and Ida Lupino in *High Sierra* (1941); she played the sweetheart of Gary Cooper in *Sergeant York* (1941) and James Cagney in *Yankee Doodle Dandy* (1942), and she danced with Fred Astaire in *The Sky's the Limit* (1943). But time was not her friend, and the size of her roles decreased when she left her teens.

At twenty-eight she was filming grade-B westerns for Republic. In a futile attempt to be tough instead of sweet, she co-starred and dueled with Audrey Totter in *The Woman They Almost Lynched* (1953), a picture that director Allan Dwan has described as a parody, though its actors and, indeed, Herbert Yates, believed that they were making a serious film. In an interview with Peter Bogdanovich, Dwan described his approach:

BOGDANOVICH: Did you tell the actors what they were doing?
DWAN: No—then they'd try to be funny. You tell some of those characters, "This is a very funny scene," they'd horse it up, put things in. But imagine—we had a gun fight between two gals—going down the street like the cowpunchers. If they'd had anything but skirts on, I'd have shot between their legs. I couldn't do that with girls. Of course, today they would strip for it.

Further Republic pictures, all in 1954, *Flight Nurse, Jubilee Trail,* and *Hell's Outpost,* simply confirmed the fact that Joan Leslie, like Ann

Rutherford, possessed a charm inseparable from youth.

She retired from films in 1956.

### Audrey Totter

Audrey Totter is a nuclear-powered actress, who, following stage and radio experience, invaded movies with *Main Street After Dark* (1944), a sprightly melodrama about a mother who trains her sons in the art of picking pockets, a kind of female Fagin from *Oliver Twist.* Selena Royle excelled as the mother, but Audrey revealed both power and promise. When Robert Montgomery selected her for his own production of *Lady in the Lake* (1946), playing her lover though never seen on the screen—in effect, identifying himself with the camera—*Esquire* announced that he had "made a star of his leading lady" (but warned her to avoid her Bette Davis mannerisms). Metro-Goldwyn-Mayer, its Mrs. Miniver and Madame Curie in rapid decline, tried to advance her career with wide publicity. The public, however, never accepted her as a star, in spite of important roles in later pictures like *The Saxon Charm* (1948), which reunited her with Montgomery and co-starred Susan Hayward. Hardboiled actresses, handsome rather than beautiful, have sometimes reached the top—Barbara Stanwyck and Bette Davis among them—but they have always managed to suggest the woman beneath the masculine mask. Women could identify, men could imagine falling in love with them, at least falling for them. As for Audrey Totter, she seemed the kind of a crony a man would take on a hike or a hunt, but not to share a sleeping bag. She was perfectly cast in Republic's *The Woman They Almost Lynched* (1953), in which she played a bandit who could outgun any man in town. But the low-budget picture did not deserve such explosive acting, and *Man or Gun* (1958) for the same studio, one of its last pictures, was equally undistinguished.

She appeared in the ill-fated television series "Our Man Higgins" (1962) and played supporting roles in *The Carpetbaggers* (1964) and *Chubasco* (1968) and many other films. In television she played the continuing role of a nurse in "Medical Center." Her power is undiminished but she continues to lack an essential ingredient to become a star: femininity.

### Evelyn Keyes

From her role as Scarlett's sister in *Gone with*

Evelyn Keyes.

Glenn Ford and Evelyn Keyes in *The Desperadoes*.

*the Wind,* she seemed to be destined to star. Ornamental in her earliest films, she grew both prettier and livelier, and she hit her stride as the wily, amorous genie in *A Thousand and One Nights* (1945). When estranged from his Princess Beautiful, Adele Jergens, Cornel Wilde resorted to his lamp, and the warmth he found consoled him for Adele. Columbia rewarded her with the coveted female lead in *The Jolson Story* (1946), a character reminiscent of Ruby Keeler, and Evelyn, with the picture, was a hit.

She had reached her peak. Her decline was unaccountable but undeniable, with *Hell's Half Acre* (Republic, 1954) close to the end. Critics who noticed the picture could only find praise for the Honolulu locations and shake their heads at the waste of an unfaded star.

Retired from films since supporting Marilyn Monroe in *The Seven-Year Itch* (1954), she has written an autobiography and married Artie Shaw.

### Angie Dickinson

Angie Dickinson, wife of composer Burt Bacharach, has made little news in recent years; at least, until she appeared as the star of the runaway television series "Police Woman," in 1974 and looked so daffodil-pretty that watchers marveled at her admitted age of forty-four. The same year, to affirm a figure as youthful as her face, she starred as *Big Bad Mama,* a picture in which she stripped and copulated as often as she killed, and brandished her breasts as if they were pistols.

Where had she been before her "instant success?"

Angie Dickinson entered movies in *Lucky Me* (1954) with Doris Day, filmed a series of low-grade

westerns, among them *The Black Whip* (1956) with Adele Mara and an atrocity for Republic, *Hidden Guns* (1956), but seemed on the verge of stardom when she supported John Wayne in *Rio Bravo* (1959) and looked so delectable that she did not have to act.

Her subsequent films include *Ocean's 11* (1960) with Frank Sinatra and his rat pack, *Captain Newman, M.D.* (1963) with Gregory Peck and Tony Curtis, and *Point Blank* (1965) with Lee Marvin (in which she replaced Kim Novak, who refused a salary of a hundred thousand dollars). After her marriage to Bacharach in 1965, she concentrated on being a wife and mother, but her guest appearance in one episode of "Police Story" (1973-) led to a spin-off and her own successful series, which now outdraws its parent in the Nielson ratings.

### Adele Jergens

Adele Jergens, the Champagne Blonde, was born to star. A Powers model before she was eighteen, she sang and danced in the chorus of Broadway musicals—*Jubilee Trail* (1935), *Dubarry Was a Lady* (1939), and others—and finally attempted Hollywood. After a fruitless year at Twentieth-Century Fox, she returned to Broadway as understudy to Gypsy Rose Lee in *Star and Garter.* A press agent might have invented the following events. When Gypsy took to her bed, Adele took her place on the stage, and what she revealed delighted a Columbia talent scout into signing her to a contract with Harry Cohn. Cohn was having his usual problems with Rita Hayworth. He needed a threat to keep her in line, a possible replacement. Rita's singing was dubbed; Adele could sing for herself. She could also dance, and her statuesque body and classical features recalled a Praxiteles Aphrodite. To give her experience before the cameras, he found her a minor role in *Together Again* with Irene Dunne, starred her in the western serial *Black Arrow,* and straightaway launched her with a huge campaign in *A Thousand and One Nights,* an Arabian extravaganza with Cornel Wilde for heroics and Evelyn Keyes for humor (playing a genie later imitated by Barbara Eden). "A new glamor item has been added to the Columbia lot," announced the publicity department, and Adele proved glamorous—a "torrid beauty," according to *Time*—and surprisingly fun in the straight role of the princess. She spoke her lines with conviction, but her mischievous eyes seemed to say, "I'm really a showgirl pretending to royalty."

Adele Jergens sings.

Adele Jergens with Cornel Wilde in Columbia's *A Thousand and One Nights* (Evelyn Keyes is the wistful genie).

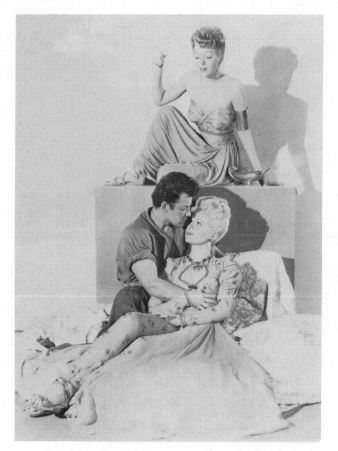

Adele Jergens on the town.

Adele Jergens with Cornel Wilde in *A Thousand and One Nights*.

Adele Jergens as the Princess Armina in *A Thousand and One Nights*.

Arthur Lake and Adele Jergens in Columbia's *Blondie's Anniversary*.

Cornel Wilde and Adele Jergens in *A Thousand and One Nights*.

Adele Jergens playing Marilyn Monroe's mother in Columbia's *Ladies of the Chorus*.

Blonde Adele Jergens goes brunette.

Edward Everett Horton, Adele Jergens, and Marc Platt in Columbia's *Down to Earth.*

Cornel Wilde and Adele Jergens in *A Thousand and One Nights.*

Cornel Wilde and Adele Jergens in *A Thousand and One Nights.*

Cornel Wilde and Adele Jergens in *A Thousand and One Nights.*

Cornel Wilde and Adele Jergens in *A Thousand and One Nights.*

Adele Jergens in Warner Brothers' *Sugarfoot.*

Cornel Wilde and Adele Jergens in *A Thousand and One Nights.*

Cornel Wilde and Adele Jergens in *A Thousand and One Nights.*

Adele Jergens.

**Adele Jergens in *A Thousand and One Nights*.**

**Adele Jergens in *A Thousand and One Nights*.**

The picture delighted critics as well as public, and Adele was an instant favorite with servicemen (the year was 1945), who deluged the young actress with proposals of marriage—and less honorable arrangements—and even composed a jingle:

Lusty
Busty,
And ready to wed.

(The "less honorable" substituted "bed" for "wed.")

But Rita turned docile and Adele was reduced to playing the bad girl in Miss Hayworth's *Down to Earth* (1947). Singing "I put the ants in the dancers' pants," she threatened to steal the show, but Cohn had typed her as a temptress—she was later to play a succession of seductive disreputables—gun molls, schemers, and husband-stealers—her face a carefully sculptured mask of rouge, lipstick, and powder.

Warren Meyers in *Who Is That?* ranks her among the Other Women: "They may have been unloveable, but they certainly appeared to have captured the hearts of their makeup men, and in their lacquered perfection, they often resembled the sinister blossoms of some forbidden plant which enchants and then enslaves the weak and the unwary." She played such roles to perfection, though in private life she was natural, modest, and altogether delightful — still ambitious to become a star, but preferring to be a total woman. After she left Columbia, she continued her shady ladies for want of better offers except on rare occasions such as Patricia Neal's suspension from Warner Brothers: a pampered star at the time, Miss Neal refused to accept the lead in a medium-budget western with Randolph Scott and Raymond Massey, *Sugarfoot* (1951), and Adele was offered the role. Breaking an old stereotype, she played a dancehall singer with an unexpected and refreshing modesty, singing her own songs and, wonder of wonders for her profession, preserving her honor for marriage. *Newsweek* called her "lovely," implying more than looks.

She free-lanced through the fifties, always giving her best, but never given the best, and shortly before she retired from the screen, she starred as—what else?—a one-time stripper in Republic's *The Beginning of the End* (1957): those who survive an atomic holocaust as humans are confronted by once-human grasshoppers eight feet tall with appetites to match their size. The picture is little regarded by science fiction fans, who point to the lack of originality in its plot and the lacklustre

Adele Jergens.

acting by Peter Graves, Lori Nelson, and the late Peggie Castle. It is almost forgotten by the general public. But Adele's performance is a miracle of acting over material. Trapped in an old house with other survivors, she recalls the days of her stardom as a stripper, the footlights, the applause, and (unlike Hayworth's Gilda) without removing so much as a single glove, re-enacts the experience to cheer her friends. It is probably her finest scene in any film. After the grasshoppers, one of whom used to be Lori Nelson's sweetheart, devour her for dinner, the picture descends to low-budget melodrama, if not to the ludicrous. But the girl who was born to star but forced to play dames, has played a dame who is worth a dozen ladies.

Adele Jergens was probably the most beautiful—some would prefer Ilona Massey—and certainly the most gifted of Republic's asteroids; for once, however, Yates cannot be blamed for neglecting to offer a contract. Adele was forty. Republic was near collapse. Her failure to attain the stardom she deserved is attributable to Columbia's Harry Cohn. When Rita began to fade, he groomed Kim Novak to take her place, and Kim proved at best an adequacy, with a short and unspectacular reign. Yet at one time, in one picture, *Ladies of the Chorus,* Cohn had under contract two inimitable and incandescent blondes, Adele Jergens and Marilyn Monroe. Fortunately, he dropped Marilyn's contract in time for her to move to Twentieth-Century Fox and become the last and the greatest of the Love Goddesses; unfortunately, he renewed Adele's contract with further promises, unfulfilled, and largely wasted her gifts.

*The Beginning of the End* was close to the end of Adele's career. After a brief foray into television, she retired to a house in the San Fernando Valley with her husband of many years, actor Glenn Langan, whom she met while filming *Treasure of Monte Cristo* in 1949, and their young son, Tracy. She received an article in *Whatever Became of . . .?, Fifth Series,* but no one has need for concern. Adele can adapt; that is her genius. She dreamed high but half was enough, both for her and her legion of fans.

## Mari Blanchard

Mari Blanchard: looks, talent, and one lucky break—these could have made her a major star. She had the looks—to spare—and the talent to match. But all of her breaks were bad. In Burt Lancaster's *Ten Tall Men* (1951), her part was chiefly confined to a stroll down the street of a Foreign Legion town. A petite and piquant blonde, twirling a parasol and smiling an invitation to the whole of the Legion, she proved irresistible to her delighted audience, and Universal Pictures rewarded her three years later with a co-starring role in *Veils of Baghdad.* Unfortunately, she blackened her locks to suit her part, and, though still attractive, she was also resistible. Fetchingly blonde again for *Rails into Laramie* (1954), she offered the best reason for riding the rails to a one-horse town, and stardom seemed in view. Lancaster, co-producing and starring with Gary Cooper in a blockbuster western, *Vera Cruz,* wanted her for his feminine lead. But Universal, aware of its valuable property, refused to allow her to accept the role. She was rare among actresses of the day in the fact that she always answered her own fan mail—generally, stars and starlets resorted to form replies from studio secretaries—and she corresponded with me through the middle fifties. Totally different from the sirens she played on the screen, unaffected and deeply affecting in her courageous acceptance of her disappointments, she wrote (March 23, 1954):

Dear Thomas:
It was so nice hearing from you again, and such a nice letter. It is gratifying to know that you have so many friends when you need them. Yes, losing the part in "Vera Cruz" was painful, but everything is for the best even though it is hard to understand. I wonder if you really know how much I appreciate your kind wishes and thoughts, but of course an actress soon realizes how much her public must mean to her.
My very best to you.
Siempre,
Mari
Mari Blanchard

Even at Universal she was kept from work for a time by an injury to her leg, sustained in a fall. But the long-awaited break appeared to have come when she was cast with Audie Murphy in a 1955 remake of *Destry Rides Again.* Murphy, still at the height of his boyish charm (and still remembered for his heroism in World War II), satisfied those who had seen James Stewart in the classic of 1939. But Mari, hoping to avoid comparisons with the incomparable Dietrich, or perhaps at the urging of her studio bosses, returned her hair to an unremarkable black. Ironically, she gave the finest performance of her career. She could turn a song into a seduction; she took a bullet intended for Murphy and died in his arms with pathos and dignity. But the darkened hair, far from avoiding harsh comparisons, had simply denied her

Jane Withers.

June Havoc.

Dietrich's gold and also confused her fans. Universal failed to renew her contract.

She played the feminine lead in the short-lived television series "Klondike," and made a number of low-budget movies for minor studios. Republic's *No Place To Land* involved her with John Ireland and Gail Russell in a tasteless triangle about a crop-duster and his entanglements with women. The film was a sad monument to the moribund careers of two once-rising actresses.

Mari Blanchard died of cancer at the age of forty-three.

Jane Withers.

*    *    *    *    *

Other starlets, other asteroids, undeserving of separate entries in view of their work for Yates, starred for Republic from time to time. Jane Withers, sixteen, after she had grown too old to torment Shirley Temple but long before she had fattened into Josephine the Plumber, played in a mini-musical, *Johnny Doughboy* (1942), which made her audience wish for the bad little girl. Marsha Hunt, a reliable supporting actress for many years, presumed to star in a 1948 comedy, *The Inside Story,* and quickly reverted to featured roles. Ella Raines, though starred with Brian Donlevy and Forrest Tucker in *The Fighting U.S. Coast Guard* (1951), seemed more at ease on the range, and in better films for bigger studios. June Havoc appeared with James Mason in *Lady Possessed* (1952), the tale of a woman who thinks herself controlled by the will of Mason's wife, one of Republic's occasional forays into the—apparently—supernatural. But Miss Havoc, as always, was haunted—and eclipsed—by another ghost, that of her famous sister, Gypsy Rose Lee. Arlene Whelan, well-groomed but wooden throughout the forties, appeared with small conviction in John Ford's convincing if low-budget tribute to the American countryside, *The Sun Comes Up* (1953), the director's personal favorite of his nearly two hundred films. Mala Powers, a fetching Roxane in United Artists' *Cyrano de Bergerac* (1950), proved an inept comedienne in a trifle called *Geraldine* (1953).

Poor, acceptable, superior, they ran the gamut, these perpetual starlets, these would-be stars, and Republic gave them a richer variety of roles than most of the public remembers. Yates, the dreamer, often liked what he saw. But Yates, the economist, failed to act upon their successes, to sign them to long-term contracts, to promote and publicize.

But another Adele was making her own way to stardom.

# 6 The Southern Star

Herbert Yates envisioned little Republic as a series of kingdoms, and its ruling stars as kings and queens of various territory. Though sometimes nicknamed "Duke," John Wayne was the undisputed king of major productions; and his queen in the eyes of kingmaker Yates was Vera Ralston,* who happily starred with Wayne in two westerns and, if Yates could have had his way, would have been Wayne's inseparable co-star in almost every film.

But Republic's smaller pictures, which greatly outnumbered the major productions, also required their rulers, and thus, thanks in part to publicity, thanks in part to backbreaking work on the part of the stars, Yates could proclaim first Gene Autry, then Roy Rogers as the "king of the singing western"; Linda Stirling as the "best of the serial queens"; and, on the face of things, the unlikeliest actress ever to act, much less aspire to rule, Judy Canova as the "hillbilly queen."

Born in Jacksonville, Florida (1916), to a family of vaudevillians, Judy nourished a schoolgirl's typical dream: to become a movie star. Her chances at best appeared inplausible, at worst impossible. In school she was the kind of girl of whom it is said, in view of her figure and face, "she has a good personality," and taken on blind dates by popular friends who want no competition. In truth, she was exceptionally plain, with a face like that of a good-natured ass, and, so it must have seemed to the local boys, no more intelligence.

But Judy, far from asinine like her face, was fully as bright as she was ambitious. The question was how to fulfill her ambitions. In the early thirties, beauties and singers went to Hollywood and hoped to be seen or heard by a studio president or a powerful producer, Louis B. Mayer or David Selznick, or at least a talent scout. Judy, knowing her physical limitations, studied classical singing, only to learn that she had no gift for what is usually considered song: patterned, melodious sounds produced by trained vocal chords. She could only claim volume. Undaunted, she chose another approach and toured in vaudeville with her parents. The training proved invaluable; a theatrical alchemist, she learned to transform her liabilities into virtues. Plainness became, when she chose, engaging homeliness. Inadequate singing became a horrendous screech. She had an ardent wish, but she knew that a wish that becomes reality is the child of patience and work: patience that never tires and indefatigable work.

Arriving in Hollywood, she found herself a crow in a bevy of meadow larks. But Judy observed a heartening fact: *the larks were overabundant, the crow was unique.* At the age of nineteen she appeared in *Going Highbrow* (1935), a trifle for Warner Brothers with Zasu Pitts and Edward Everett Horton. Her role was slight and largely ignored. But later in the year, Busby Berkeley, he of the lavish productions and the intricate songs and dances, perhaps the greatest of Hollywood's musical masters, cast her, unbilled, in a top-budget musical, *In Caliente,* starring the popular Mexican actress, Dolores Del Rio. The lack of billing was

---

*To most of the public, she was simply the "queen of the Bs."

Judy Canova.

not an affront, for the perspicacious Berkeley had recognized Judy's gifts. In a scene of consummate style, in a gown that might have been tailored for Marion Davies and charged to the checking account of William Randolph Hearst, she appeared to the total astonishment of her audience and proceeded to butcher a song called "The Lady in Red." Her sound might be called a barnyard medley, part hog-grunt, part rooster-crow, part caterwaul.

She stole the picture from Miss Del Rio and became a minor celebrity. Still, she was hard to cast. She had to wait. For two years she waited with humor, courage, and expectation. In 1937 she supported those rising sirens Betty Grable and Dorothy Lamour in *Thrill of a Lifetime;* and the same year she appeared with Jack Benny and Ida Lupino in *Artists and Models.* Audiences loved her in lesser roles—her barnyard numbers were a jaunty surprise among the glamorous offerings of the stars: pigtailed Judy and Dorothy Lamour, newly synonymous with the sarong; shapeless Judy and Betty Grable, the shapely wriggler. But no major studio offered her leads. Moviegoers at large enjoyed a novelty number, and Judy was raucous, unconventional, and diverting; but they wanted fabulous stars to carry the stories and comical starlets for interludes. It was Judy's place to amuse; Judy was comic relief in the old tradition of Falstaff in *Henry VI.*

The time to wait had ended; the time to act was at hand. She had not come to Hollywood to support the Lamours and the Grables; she had come to star. Her place, she decided, was a lesser studio, in lesser pictures that could play the hinterlands; there she could have the leads; there she could be a "hillbilly queen." In 1940, at the age of twenty-four, she was quick to accept an offer from Herbert Yates. Judy was not in the least his ideal woman—he was waiting for cosmopolitan Vera to enter his life—but he knew his audience and his economics. Judy in turn had no illusions about her skill or what it meant to star in low-budget films. She had faced a choice: remain a featured player, an oddity such as Carmen Miranda, introduced in the same year by Twentieth-Century Fox (*Down Argentine Way*); or star in films on Poverty Row, for a studio chiefly known for its westerns and serials and, til now, its neglect of actresses. She had made a wise decision. Supported by Eddie Foy, Jr., one of the Seven Little Foys,* she became a star in her first Republic film, *Scatterbrain* (1940).

From 1940 to 1955, she starred in thirteen movies for Republic. Her pictures were almost indistinguishable in plot; her performances, which included yodeling as well as barnyard singing, and possibly calling hogs, never varied from her established type. Whether she played a North Carolina Hillbilly, a Florida Cracker, or a hayseed from Louisiana, she remained, unalterably and hilariously, Judy Canova. She was the country girl, plain, put-upon, but enduring; city-folk were the suave, unscrupulous villains. She was the sleepytime Cinderella who won her prince and silenced her arrogant sisters without the help of a fairy godmother's wand, and without the need (or the face) to emerge as a storybook princess. Republic's serials appealed to men and boys, but Judy's pictures lured the wives along with the husbands, the sisters along with the brothers, and their short filming schedules, their juvenile plots, their trite dialogue, were quickly forgotten when Judy opened her mouth. What is more, they did not require expensive advertisement, press books, interviews, or promotional tours. Judy's name was the draw. To Republic, they became what the Andy Hardy pictures were to Metro-Goldwyn-Mayer.

In *Sis Hopkins* (1941), countrified Judy, visiting a rich uncle, enrolls at a finishing school for girls, among them a little known starlet, Susan Hayward. Judy's snobbish schoolmates make her the butt of their jokes, but Judy retaliates with the help of Bob Crosby, and native honesty triumphs over citified wiles. In *Thrill of a Lifetime,* plain Judy had been a foil to voluptuous Grable and lithe Lamour; in *Artists and Models,* to Ida Lupino, imported from England for her waiflike charms. Now, the tables are turned. Ravishing Hayward becomes a foil to Judy; sophistication yields to naturalness.

In *Joan of Ozark* (1942), not only is Judy co-starred with Joe E. Brown, a popular star with circus and vaudeville training, she is given such able supporting players as Eddie Foy, Jr., Jerome Cowan, and Ann Jeffreys.* Instead of city slickers, it is wily Nazi spies with whom she matches wits, but bumbling Judy, straight from the Ozarks and coifed in pigtails with peppermint-striped bows, is more than their match.

*Chatterbox* (1943) reunited her with Joe E. Brown, and the comic styles of the pair were so remarkably similar that they were hailed by their fans as a rusticated version of Katharine Hepburn

*A family theatrical team that inspired a movie with Bob Hope.

*Miss Jeffreys, trained in opera, achieved renown in musicals on the New York stage, and later on television, opposite her husband, Robert Sterling, in "Topper" (1953).

and Spencer Tracy, whose *Woman of the Year* was appearing in major cities while *Chatterbox* played in the sticks. Both Judy and Joe used their generous mouths and their long, rubbery faces to comic effect. Top-billed Judy was louder than Joe; Joe made more of his lines—all in all, they formed a perfect team.

Picture followed picture in quick succession, averaging one a year for Republic, and little Columbia, still among the minors, borrowed Judy for three of its musicals but wisely retained the successful formula. No one asked that Judy Canova become a Lucille Ball, whose roles have ranged from the callous nightclub singer of *The Big Street* (1942), through the irrepressible Lucy of television, through the movie madcap, Mame. In fact, part of Judy's appeal was her predictability. A change in style might have proved as disconcerting as Phyllis Diller's facelift, and as damaging to her career.

As Republic entered the fifties and audiences grew more demanding, she began to lose her appeal. After 1955 and *Lay That Rifle Down,* her weakest film, with her weakest co-star in Robert Lowery, she retired from the screen, except for a cameo role in Metro-Goldwyn-Mayer's *Adventures of Huckleberry Finn* (1960). Wisely, however, she had paralleled her pictures with a popular radio show and frequent guest appearances on television and become, in fact, a millionaire. In 1957 she formed her own Television Production Company, Inc., but found that, whatever the audience, movie or video, people had tired of her broad humor and the entourage she had gathered through the years, Pedro, Cousin Ureenus, who thrived on chopped liver ice cream, and other sylvan oddballs. Eclipsed in movies, she was even less in demand on television, which accentuated her brash mannerisms and, within the intimacies of the living room, caricatured a caricature.

Practical Judy had fulfilled her dream; she did not try to prolong her fading career, but retired with her family—her second husband and two daughters—to a mansion in the San Fernando Valley. Her palatial home was close to that of Herbert Yates and Vera Ralston. Thus, two of Yates's queens lived side by side; Judy real but modest; Vera grand but synthetic; the one who had made for her studio a minor fortune in little pictures, the other who had lost for her studio a major fortune in large disasters.

The average length of movie stardom is five years. Judy's Republic stardom lasted fifteen years. What were the reasons for the long success of so unlikely an actress? Perhaps she can be compared

to a good country ballad. The words are simple and often stale; verses repetitious; delivery nasal. And yet there is something about such a song that makes it unforgettable to many listeners. Judy, like the ballad, appealed to a pair of deeply entrenched American myths:

1. Country people are better than city people; the city, that asphalt jungle, that neon wilderness, hardens men; living among the fields allows their essential goodness to flower along with their crops.
2. A farmer is more than a match for a city slicker (and most city-dwellers are slick); wisdom comes from the earth along with goodness; machines, not truths, are the products of city life.

Judy, epitomizing the country, added another appeal: unpretension. Without the curls and the curves of a Daisy Mae, plainer than most of the women in her audience, she aroused compassion instead of contempt; understanding laughter instead of snickers. Apparently equipped for nothing more admirable than calling hogs, she managed not only survival but success; she offered hope for the homely, and the seemingly talentless—*if Judy can do it, why not me?*

The city girl looked to Crawford who, born Lucille le Sueur, shy, awkward, poorly educated, had gone to Hollywood and become a star. The farm girl looked to Judy and took heart from her surprising achievement; yes, and envied her, with her long face and her big mouth, in her little films with their clumsy plots, for Judy, even as Joan, had become a star.

It is true that most of her movies are badly dated by 1975. The myth of agrarian innocence and rural wisdom had dwindled along with the countryside. Other, more able comediennes—Carol Burnett, Lili Tomlin—have taken their cue from Judy and made a virtue of homeliness, but added the full range of a comic's skills. "The Beverly Hillbillies," in its seven-year run on television (1962-69), gathered assorted and versatile talents—Buddy Ebsen, Irene Ryan—into a rustic menage, and achieved a variety lacking in Judy's unvaried performances.

Today, however, she is still fondly remembered by older people, and recognized, if not always appreciated, by the young who watch the late, late show. Richard Lamparski wrote an appealing account of her in *Whatever Became of . . . ?* (1967), and as lately as 1975, she received a short but affectionate article in *Star Quality,* a book that was simultaneously published in America and

England. Those who meet her in person find her gray-haired but chic, and not in the least like the young hayseed with the strident voice. The hillbilly queen, though she ruled a minor kingdom, exercised real power. And the dowager queen has lost her homeliness and matured into stunning grace.

# 7 The Star That Failed To Rise

Harry Cohn, better remembered as King Cohn, the late president of Columbia Pictures, proudly insisted that he could make an unknown grandmother into a star. There was a certain truth behind the exaggeration: if not a grandmother, at least Kim Novak. When Rita Hayworth began to lose both her looks and her fans, he selected Kim, an unknown starlet, to take her place. His cosmeticians styled a pretty girl into a beautiful woman. His acting coaches taught her to read her lines with a certain pathetic charm, to walk with languor, and to look inscrutable, even if not to act. He cast the beauteous Kim with the fading Rita in *Pal Joey,* and Kim became a star.

Herbert Yates was considerably less fortunate with Vera Hruba Ralston (but then, Miss Ralston was considerably less lovely than Kim Novak, and, if possible, less talented).

Her reviews were always bad:

> She quickly won a deserved reputation as the most stiff and amateurish performer who ever starred in pictures. —*The Shooting Star; A Biography of John Wayne.*

> It required the immense "pulling power" of a John Wayne to aid Miss Ralston's career whenever feasible, for she was an inept actress. —*Starring John Wayne.*

> After all, Vera Hruba Ralston was a large woman, who really didn't look graceful on ice skates. A Czechoslovakian skating champion she may have been, but over here in the United States she just wasn't any screen competition for Sonja Henie. —*Hollywood's Poverty Row.*

> She could be considered, at best, Wayne's least effective leading lady in his long career of major films. —*John Wayne: A Pyramid Illustrated History of the Movies.*

> In spite of backing by Yates, Vera Ralston never became a true star. Everything possible was done for her but she was never able to overcome the limitations of her own small talent and beauty. Today there are few film fans who even recall her name. —*Forty Years in Hollywood.*

Her many pictures were for the most part so mediocre, if not downright abominable, that any account of her years at Republic must concentrate on her relationship with President Yates rather than her performances. She was first his mistress, later his wife, and the manner in which she achieved her position and became, in the eyes of her lover, a "star," is whimsical rather than sordid.

During the thirties Vera Hruba, using her maiden name and still in her teens, won a certain fame as a skating champion in Europe. The daughter of a Czechoslovakian jewel merchant, she fled with her mother to England in 1938, anticipating the war and the German invasion of her defenseless country. Adding the name "Ralston" in order to sound less foreign to the conservative British, she skated in ice revues with moderate success. But moderation did not fulfill her hopes: the same year, she sailed to America with the expectation of entering movies like Sonja Henie, whose Barbie-doll face and agile feet had quickly made her a star. Vera was no Sonja except in youth, but she caught the eye of aging President Yates in a show called

**Vera Ralston.**

*Ice-Capades.* Though forty years her senior, he fell in love with a schoolboy's ardor—and a tycoon's wherewithal. He promptly bought the movie rights to the show, and Vera skated in her first two films, *Ice-Capades* (1941) and *Ice-Capades Revue* (1942). Speaking little, skating much, she did not need to act.

She was a disciplined athlete, an attractive woman, but she had no skill as an actress and no one could call her remotely beautiful. Nevertheless, she contrived to become a star. She agreed to be Yates's mistress if he would make her Republic's leading lady. Compared to Judy Canova, his hillbilly queen, she looked like a Byzantine empress. Happily he agreed, and he hurried to move her into his San Fernando mansion. Having been strictly raised by old-country morals, she showed a touch of propriety lacking in the sordid affairs of Louis B. Mayer and the actresses he seduced on the sly with a promise to make them stars. She invited her mother to be her companion.

Ensconced in elegant sin, she awaited her promised reward. Yates had convinced himself that he had not bought a mistress but found a star of incomparable magnitude, and he planned a campaign to bring her to public acclaim. In actual life, she was a large, muscular woman with shoulders almost as broad as those of John Wayne (or so Wayne liked to joke). Her small, close-set eyes, her thin features, sparkled with quick intelligence but not with beauty, and they seemed misplaced atop the rugged frame. She did possess a flattering camera angle: three-quarters view, head turned to the right. And careful styling in clothes and hair also improved her appearance. Her photographs from this particular angle, which magnify the minimal nose and seem to separate the eyes by a suitable space, reveal a woman to fill Yates's dream, and the public, which had overlooked her in the two revues, was led to expect an equivalent face on the screen in a costly horror film, preceded by a large promotion, *The Lady and the Monster.* Erich Von

Stroheim played a demented scientist who perpetuated a brain when its body had died and gradually lost his own identity to his "victim." (The later, more frightening version with Lew Ayres was titled *Donovan's Brain,* 1953.) Miss Ralston was only required to scream and flutter her eyes, and the public had no chance to assess her as an actress. However, she was carelessly photographed; that is to say, the cameramen, unlike those who worked for the major studios and followed the whims of the leading ladies (beware of Claudette Colbert if you shot her "bad" profile), did not limit their shots to flattering angles. Action photographers, they emphasized the monster and neglected the lady, and the thin nose dividing the small eyes was naked to public view on the large screen. Furthermore, her blonde hair was frizzled like that of Elsa Lanchester in *The Bride of Frankenstein* (or was she wearing a fright wig?). Perhaps the effect was appropriate to the picture, but it did not become the star. Moviegoers conjectured: which was the lady and which was the monster? Except for Yates, her career would have ended with her first nonskating role.

But Yates was persistent as well as besotted. He engaged meticulous cosmeticians and assured becoming camera angles for her next film, *Storm Over Lisbon* (1944), and the result was a woman at least attractive if short of pretty—the offscreen woman, in fact—though her acting had not improved; indeed, it was indiscernible. Her natural animation, her lively intelligence, vanished as soon as she stepped before a camera, just as, in reverse a merely attractive Marilyn Monroe became a temptress in front of the camera and on the screen. To Marilyn, the camera was a lover. To Vera, it was an enemy. One recourse was left to make her a star: Yates decided to cast her opposite Wayne, his hottest property, in the big-budget western *Dakota* (1945). Though Vera was hailed in the ads as "the screen's most beautiful woman," the picture was unexceptional and Vera was obvious for the wrong reasons. Nevertheless, in an era when people went to see stars as well as pictures, the name of John Wayne ensured a sizable profit.

Supposing that Vera had helped to assure the success of his picture, Yates starred her in an expensive musical, *Murder in the Music Hall* (1946), without Wayne, and his art department produced an eerie, if melodramatic, ad whose caption read, "In one mad mind, this love-crazed cry—'She's too beautiful to live.'" The picture died in minor theaters.

After the war, Vera's father, the jewel merchant, traveled to California in a vain attempt to reclaim

Vera Ralston.

Vera Ralston.

Vera Ralston in Republic's *Lake Placid Serenade*.

**Fred MacMurray** in *Fair Wind to Java*.

his wife and daughter. Old-fashioned, finding her in a liaison with a man who was almost three times her age and making bad or unremarkable movies, he begged her to return to innocence in Czechoslovakia. She refused and quarreled with him, and her mother took her part. He consoled himself with a new set of dentures and returned to his Communist-controlled homeland rather than stay in America with his wife and "sinful" daughter.

Perhaps in protest against her father's rejection, Vera removed the "Hruba" from her name and continued to star in such disasters as *The Flame* (1947) and *I, Jane Doe* (1948). In both of these pictures, as in the later *Belle Le Grand* (1951), her co-star was the talented John Carroll. It has often been said that, except for resembling Clark Gable, he would have been a major star, because he could sing as well as act, and his virile looks excited the ladies. But he lacked the drawing power of a John Wayne, and he could not save the films from heavy losses. To the public, Vera Ralston had become a joke, and fellow workers, though they found her intelligent and likable off the screen, referred to her in private as "Vera Hruba."

Yates decided upon a further strategem (described by Maurice Zolotow in *The Shooting Star).* John Wayne, now a producer with his own company, Batjac, had bought *The Fighting Kentuckian,* a tale of Napoleon's former soldiers who fled to Kentucky in search of further adventures. He engaged a good director, ensured a polished script, and asked Yates to finance and release the film through Republic. Yates said yes: if Wayne would star Miss Ralston.

Wayne, along with most of the handsomer males on Republic's lot, had endured inordinate jealousy from Yates. His interest in Vera was not romantic; a generous man, he had given her English lessons in his dressing room and aroused the wrath of his boss. Now, though married to Chata Ceballos, he must allay suspicion by using the Czechoslovakian Ralston in a role he had meant for a soft-spoken French actress like Simone Simon, Danielle Darrieux, or Corinne Calvet. He was forced to engage additional Czechs, among them Hugo Haas for Miss Ralston's father, so that her heavy accent would not obtrude and spoil her scenes. The finished picture, including Oliver Hardy for comic relief, was a great commercial success with artistic flaws. The biggest flaw was Ralston.*

Yates's uxorious tactics rankled Wayne. Rarely a critic's favorite, he wanted good reviews as well as fame. When he suggested that he produce an additional film, concerned with David Crockett and the fall of the Alamo, Yates was enthusiastic—if Wayne would star Miss Ralston. But Wayne, realizing that she would prove disastrous to a multimillion-dollar project in which there were no large roles even for accomplished actresses, quickly postponed the film. (In 1960, as producer, director, and star, he financed the picture for twelve million dollars and, even without the impediment of Miss Ralston, lost much of his personal fortune, which he later recovered by re-releases and a sale to television.) He made a final picture for Republic, *The Quiet Man* (1952), with its Irish heroine, impossible for a Czech, superbly played by Maureen O'Hara, and then he produced and acted for bigger companies. Thus, to a large extent, Miss Ralston and the importunities of her lover had been responsible for the loss of Republic's greatest star, its best defense against the encroachment of televison.

In 1950 some of Yates's militant stockholders protested his "starring" of a talentless woman and claimed that Miss Ralston was driving the studio into bankruptcy. They charged that all of her films, except for the two which she had made with Wayne, had lost a fortune and alienated critics, and the worst of them, *Angel on the Amazon* (1948), in spite of its able co-stars, George Brent and Brian Aherne,* the fantasy of a woman like Haggard's *She,* resembled a twelve-episode serial spliced into feature length. Yates not only overruled their objections, he cast his "maligned" mistress in *Belle Le Grand,* one of her silliest pictures and Republic's biggest losers.

Finally, in March 1952, Yates and his mistress of more than eleven years were married in a simple if somewhat belated ceremony; he was seventy-two; she was almost thirty-two; and in 1953, though Republic was losing its struggle with television, he rewarded his wife with her best picture since *The Fighting Kentuckian: Fair Wind to Java.* Black-haired, adorned with pearls and decked in a Dorothy Lamour sarong, she almost seemed to act because her co-star, Fred McMurray, was so ill at ease as a sea captain battling a pirate that he forgot to act, and the exciting adventure scenes—chases by land and sea, naval engagements, explosions—allowed the stars to abide and not obtrude as colorfully costumed mannequins. Republic's

**Vera Ralston in *Lake Placid Serenade*.**

**Vera Ralston in *Lake Placid Serenade*.**

miniature department constructed a twelve-foot schooner steered by a hidden man and propelled by an underwater cable. California's own Lake

Mono more than sufficed for the South Seas. Furthermore, though Vera was now thirty-two, she revealed the remarkable fact that, like the heroine of *Angle on the Amazon,* she scarcely seemed to have aged. An attractive young woman remained attractive and young.

Yates continued to star his wife until the demise of his studio, releasing her final movies, *The Notorious Mr. Monks* and *The Man Who Died Twice,* in 1958. No other studio offered her scripts—she never made a picture except for Republic—and the pair lived in prosperous retirement until the death of Yates in 1966 at the age of eighty-six. Vera's grief was real; it was not until 1974 that she married a second time.

The March-February romance reads at times like a comic opera. It is true that she was neither a beauty nor an actress, and that her movies, with few exceptions, were boring, overblown, and commercially unsuccessful. It is also true that Yates, a lonely, aging man who had dedicated his youth and middle years to making a fortune, found in her the ideal companion, the rarest of inspirations. Perhaps it was she who inspired the maker of Saturday westerns to *Johnny Guitar* and *The Red Pony*. At any rate, she served as a charming hostess to his friends; she proved a devoted mistress, a faithful wife. Unlike Marion Davies, who liked to seduce her co-stars even while living with Hearst, she did not accept her patron's love and then cavort with the young. She became his confidante in business decisions, and her quick mind, her powerful will, enabled her to advise him well in many instances. The agreement she made with Yates possessed its own morality. To our free-living seventies, her bringing her mother into her lover's house presents a nostalgic charm. Nor can she really be blamed for thinking herself a beauty when she saw the stills by Roman Freulich or heard the compliments of an adoring lover.

Her one mistake—shared and compounded by Yates—was an unshakable belief in herself as an actress and her steadfast refusal to recognize the fact that she was a liability to the studio. She had learned to become a brilliant skater in Europe. But acting, unlike skating, is a gift instead of a skill. With determination, a skill can be developed, but a gift must come with birth. (The fairy-godmother myth is founded in truth.)

Vera Ralston possessed the determination but not the gift. A footnote in the history of Hollywood, she remains the synthetic star of twenty-seven pictures.

# 8 The Evening Star

What is a star? A woman of singular beauty—a consummate actress—either or both. Easy to recognize, hard to define, a star is an image-maker and herself an image. With words and gestures, the hush in a voice, the lift of a hand, she invokes her sorcery and we, the bewitched, believe—in red shoes and a yellow brick road—in a girl with celestial visions or a woman whose sins are as bright as her name.

Garbo, Crawford, Davis—yes, and Adele Mara. Forgotten?

It is time to remember her.

\*    \*    \*    \*    \*

In the seventies Cybill Shepherd, a shapely model with no discernible talent, was given starring roles by Peter Bogdanovich, her acknowledged lover. In the forties and fifties, Vera Ralston owed her minimal fame entirely to Herbert Yates. In the twenties and thirties, the financier and publisher William Randolf Hearst purchased a spurious stardom for Marion Davies and, ignoring her natural gift for comedy, presented her as a great dramatic actress in the tradition of Bernhardt.

Adele Mara never needed a sponsor. In a career unblemished by scandal, she sang, danced, and acted with growing assurance, and, after a long apprenticeship, she became a genuine star in major productions for Republic Pictures.

Christened Adelaida Delgado, she shortened her name to the more pronounceable but no less foreign and fetching Adele Mara and began her movie career in *Navy Blues* (1941), a Warner Brothers' production with Anne Sheridan, Martha Raye, and Jackie Gleason. Adele had been born in Highland Park, Michigan (1923), and not in Spain, Hungary, Sweden, or any of the other distant and, to American audiences, mysterious countries from which such older actresses as Marlene Dietrich, Hedy Lamarr, Ingrid Bergman, and Ilona Massey were imported to Hollywood like birds of paradise. Still, her parents were Spanish American; her beauty was dark and Latin; and she richly deserved the overused adjective: exotic.

Her debut small and ignored, she moved to Columbia and caught the public eye when she sang with Xavier Cugat in *You Were Never Lovelier,* a plush musical starring Rita Hayworth and Fred Astaire. Unfortunately, instant stardom in movies has always been a myth. As we have seen, Rita had toiled for years and changed both her name and looks before she became a star with the help of Harry Cohn. According to her publicists, Jennifer Jones appeared on the scene like a genie raised from a flask by David Selznick and won an Academy Award with her first picture, *Song of Bernadette,* in 1943. A genie she might have been in her magic-making, but her real name was Phyllis Isley and she had worked for Republic in 1939.

When Adele signed with Columbia, President Cohn did not envision her as a star. His rule was tyrannical, but his kingdom was small. Columbia could only afford a single queen, and Cohn had expended a fortune on Rita's crown. Adele was signed for hard work and little recognition in low-budget features, and her publicity was con-

114

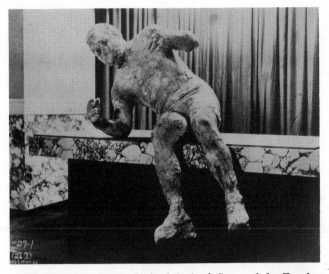

Adele Mara's co-star in United Artists' *Curse of the Faceless Man*.

Adele Mara in *Song of Mexico*.

fined to pin-ups for servicemen. (It was only after Adele's departure for Republic that the talented Miss Hayworth, recalcitrant over scripts and salary, inclined to frequent marriages and sudden retirements, infuriated her boss enough to consider replacing her.)

Adele's ten movies for Columbia were unexceptional. She went to college with Blondie (*Blondie Goes to College*, 1942), and she sprang a brother from prison with the help of Boston Blackie (*Alias Boston Blackie*, 1942), but both series continued and proliferated without her. Aside from *You Were Never Lovelier*, perhaps the low-budget *Reveille with Beverly* (1943), which starred a tap-dancing nonpariel, Ann Miller, and *Shut My Big Mouth* (1942), with Joe E. Brown, were the best of her films, though their economies showed in every aspect except the enthusiasm of their stars. As a

pin-up girl, however, she enjoyed a real and rising popularity.

When she signed a seven-year contract with Republic in 1944, America was engaged in its second World War, and servicemen had plastered their barracks walls with pictures of movie actresses to compensate for the girls they had left at home. If the pin-up queens were lovelier than the sweetest of the sweethearts, they aptly fulfilled their function as women of fantasy for men who must face a cruel reality. If not the girls he had known, they were the girls a soldier would like to know. Tacked above his bunk, they were the dreams to enfold him into sleep against a barrage of sirens and shells. Who can forget them: Rita Hayworth, nacreous in a nightgown and rising from her couch like Venus from the foam (or, to the less mythology-minded, like a temptress who has shared a night of love without mussing her hair); Betty Grable, peering an invitation over her shoulder; Lana Turner, whose sweater was not designed to keep her warm; Jane Russell in imminent danger of losing her double claims to renown; and Adele Mara, the youngest and the sauciest, in a pose that won an Academy Award for the famous Hollywood photographer Roman Freulich? Her outfit is such as to fill the dream of a cowboy as well as a soldier. She is raising two six-shooters over her head, but no one can doubt that they are meant for *them*, whether German or Japanese, and she is meant for *us*. Her cowgirl attire consists of two empty holsters, a sombrero, a bandana serving valiantly as a brassiere, trunks resembling panties, and beaded boots. The costume reveals a face and figure so ideally proportioned that it is useless to acclaim a particular region, as with Betty "The Legs" Grable or Jane "The Bosom" Russell. Academy Awards are intended for major achievements, and a true artist has photographed a living work of art. The total nudity, the instant availability of a *Playboy* centerfold, looks unimaginative in comparison.

For Republic as for Columbia, Adele toiled in picture after picture—thirty-nine in five years—and played everything from microscopic roles with John Wayne in *The Fighting Seabees* (1944) and *The Flame of the Barbary Coast* (1945), to singing cowgirls with both Gene Autrey and Roy Rogers, to the star of a miniature musical with Edgar Barrier, *Song of Mexico* (1945), to girls both good and bad in horror pictures, costume dramas, and gangster films. Unfortunately for Adele, President Yates was so enamored with Vera Ralston that he continued to cast his Czechoslovakian mistress in his biggest pictures and ordered his publicity

Joe E. Brown and the teenage Adele Mara in Columbia's *Shut My Big Mouth.*

department to concentrate on making a star of her in the public eye. Nevertheless, he personally supervised all of his pictures and Adele impressed him with her incredible jitterbug in *The Fighting Seabees,* her maturing beauty in *The Catman of Paris* (1946), and a versatility compounded of inherited talent, hard work, a gift for accents, and a face so expressive that, with a change of hair style and gown, she could suggest a callow girl or a cosmopolitan woman, a nineteenth-century Parisian or a twentieth-century collegian.

Miss Ralston's position as queen of the lot was unfortunate, but undeniable. She was, however, a queen with a faithful king but few loyal subjects; worse, she had never learned to act. Every role was beyond her range; in some, she appeared so ridiculous that even Yates must cast with care.

Sometimes he borrowed a star from another studio or looked to his ladies in waiting. Adele, it seemed, had not waited in vain.

In 1948, after four years of uncomplaining and uncompromising service, she played a minor role with Vera and Ruth Hussey in *I, Jane Doe;* she endured two westerns, a college musical, and a comedy, all of them undistinguished except for her own distinction. But two of her seven pictures in that film-filled year were notable: *Wake of the Red Witch* and *Angel in Exile.*

*Wake of the Red Witch* is the story of a ruthless sea captain and his feud with a sinister shipping magnate. John Wayne played the captain, a man who, according to the script, was as unscrupulous as the magnate. Unlike James Cagney and Humphrey Bogart, who excelled as antiheroes, Wayne had never appeared at ease in a shaded role, half heroic, half demoniac. Now, he froze his

**Adele Mara.**

sarong, was seductive but unmysterious. Adele, dancing by torchlight in similar unattire, was the quintessential mystery, woman as man imagines her in his ripest fantasies. Unforgiveably, when the film was released to the public, the dance remained on the floor of the cutting room. The leading fan magazines, formidable in that day, even as Louella Parsons and Hedda Hopper in their newspaper columns, speculated about the omission. Perhaps the original length—the picture was released at 106 minutes—had seemed too long for a time when major features were accompanied by cartoons and travelogues. Perhaps the picture displayed Miss Mara to such advantage that John Wayne, an intimate friend of Yates and, off-screen, romantically linked with Miss Russell, had requested the cut to prevent the total effacement of his protégé. Perhaps the dance was too erotic for a studio that had no wish to clash with the censors and endanger its reputation for much action and little love. The mystery remains unresolved; imagination must supply the dance; but everyone saw a star performance by a featured player.

In Adele's finest picture, they saw an even richer performance by an acknowledged star. *Angel in*

face into a single expression of mindless intensity, even when making love to Gail Russell. Misplaced in Hollywood, the shy, pretty actress failed to act, or to exact from her famous co-star the least suggestion of passion or tenderness; instead of thawing her lover, she bewildered him.

If the "stars" failed to star, however, their failure allowed the featured players, together with expert models of sailing ships and lush tropical scenery, to steal the picture. Luther Adler excelled as Wayne's nemesis, who indirectly contrived his death in a diving accident, superbly filmed by cameramen who were more accustomed to plains and buttes than to sunken wrecks. And Adele Mara not only outacted Miss Russell, who died of a lingering malaise in her one believable scene, she outlived her to enjoy a consummation with heroic Gig Young. The costumes became her beauty; named Teleia Van Schreven, dark-eyed but saffron-haired, she played a bewitching combination of Dutch and Polynesian and she heightened her witchery with an accent of no discernible origin. The script allowed her to rise mysteriously from island lagoons or materialize in a cluster of flame trees or palms. Dorothy Lamour, languorous in her

**Adele Mara and John Carroll in *Angel in Exile*.**

John Carroll and Adele Mara in *Angel in Exile.*

Carroll, hide their loot in a cave, only to have it discovered by the local townspeople and hailed as a gift from God. Adele is the "angel in exile," a peasant girl who reforms the hard-bitten Carroll and proves that the true gift is far more precious than gold. The picture, originally entitled *The Blue Lady,* was released as *Angel in Exile* because President Yates enjoyed a predilection for angels, in titles if not in women *(Angel and the Badman* with John Wayne and Gail Russell, *Angel on the Amazon* with Vera Ralston and George Brent).But the change, if less euphonious to the ear, is more appropriate to interpretations beyond the literal. Is Adele an "angel in exile" because she is an innocent girl in a free-living time and town? Or because she is truly an angel exiled from heaven to reform a rogue and his band?

The average moviegoer accepted the picture as a straightforward adventure with ironies but hardly ambiguities. Republic was not renowned for its metaphysics, its portraits of Jennie. The careful viewer, however, observed the nuances of Miss Mara's role, the tremulous gestures of a being not yet at ease in an alien place. They watched her enter the cave of the treasure—light into dark?— heaven daring hell?—with hesitation and yet with determination. They watched her emerge ecstatic

*Exile* is a minor classic, which, in spite of its running time of ninety minutes, a strong indication that it was not intended for double features, and in spite of direction by the celebrated Allan Dwan, whose career had begun with the silents and whom Andrew Sarris has called "the last of the old masters," failed in many cases to find a booking in major theaters. For the most part, it played in neighborhood houses as the upper half of a double bill, sometimes paired with *Ladies of the Chorus,* a low-budget feature from Columbia notable for the bizarre casting of the thirty-year-old Adele Jergens as the mother of the twenty-two-year-old newcomer, Marilyn Monroe. Only in 1975 has *Angel in Exile* been reevaluated by *Movies of TV* and accorded three stars and a notation, "good melodrama."

Of course, it is more than merely a melodrama and more than merely good. A melodrama is a story in which action, generally violent, takes precedence over character. A "good" melodrama makes character equal to action and avoids needless violence. But *Angel in Exile,* notwithstanding its simple plot, possesses the intimations that are the hallmark of every true classic and, like *The Song of Bernadette,* suggests more than it says.

A band of thieves on the run, headed by John

**Adele Mara as the *Angel in Exile.***

Adele Mara in *The Vampire's Ghost*.

with discovery of gold and self: a girl who is more than a peasant, she has remembered another country but accepted her exile to achieve a mission. For Miss Mara, *Angel in Exile* was more than a mission, it was the finest picture of her career.

Herbert Yates was compelled to recognize a phenomenon on his lot. With little guidance and less publicity, a young actress had climbed a ladder of unremarkable roles, rung after difficult rung, and, in one year and two pictures, become a star. If it troubled him that Adele and not Vera had proved herself the real actress and the true exotic, at least he did not punish her with lesser roles. Indeed, he rewarded her in 1949 with Republic's highest prize: a co-starring role with John Wayne in *The Sands of Iwo Jima*.

In spite of nautical tales like *Wake of the Red Witch*, Wayne was largely identified with the western, but he had attracted audiences if not critics in such World War II movies as *The Fighting Seabees, Back to Bataan, They Were Expendable*, and *The Flying Tigers*. Thus, *The Sands of Iwo Jima* was not a departure but a culmination. Directed by Allan Dwan of *Angel in Exile*, alternating vigorous action sequences with intimate glimpses into a soldier's mind, the picture presented Wayne as lifelike yet larger than life, a hard-fisted sergeant with a roar instead of a voice and a stride instead of a walk, and won him his first nomination for an Academy Award.

Reviewers, lavishing praise on Wayne, largely neglected his co-star, Adele, who played the New Zealand sweetheart of John Agar, one of Wayne's men. The movies of World War II almost invariably included a romance to attract the ladies, and too often such romances fell into stereotypes, warrior and woman exchanging kisses and coquetries

119

**Adele Mara and John Carroll in *The Avengers*.**

**Adele Mara in *The Avengers*.**

before he marches to deeds of valor and possibly death. Perhaps the pairing with Agar instead of Wayne deceived the critics into underestimating the strength of Adele's performance, her skill at finding originality in a potential platitude.

When a young, aspiring actress is given a co-starring role with a great, long-established star, she is often tempted to overplay; to make less seem more; to justify her billing. Wisely Miss Mara brought to her scenes with Agar—their meeting at a dance for servicemen, their wedding, their parting —a balance of understatement and allure. She did not attempt to mimic a "New Zealand accent," for New Zealand, like the larger United States, is a polyglot land of several races and several accents. Rather, she modulated her voice to suggest a girl like Teleia Van Schreven of no particular time or place. Particularity she reserved for the *kind* of a girl: too alluring to resist, too moral to yield before marriage. She was not the easy conquest of a

soldier's dream. She was conquerable, but with the weapon of wedded love. In a world of change and death, she was fidelity. A viewer could well regret that Agar and not Wayne should win such a bride. For Wayne, though a major star, was better known for making war than love. The westerns in which he had learned to ride hard, draw fast, and shoot straight had failed to teach him that combination of strength and tenderness that was the essence of Clark Gable or Robert Taylor or even Humphrey Bogart. Not with Gail Russell, not even with Clair Trevor, had he appeared to believe the love he spoke. In love, it seemed, the man's man was a clumsy boy. He must wait for Maureen O'Hara in *Rio Grande* and *The Quiet Man* to teach, indeed to compel, the true romantic response. Had Adele played his bride in *The Sands of Iwo Jima,* she would have proved an earlier, no less experienced teacher.

Her own performance, however, remained perfection. The picture was the most profitable and one of the most proficient ever made by Republic and Adele was justly billed as its feminine star.

In 1950 she sustained, though she did not expand, her career in three less costly but nevertheless commendable films, a historical adventure called *The Avengers* and two westerns, *California Passage* and *Rock Island Trail.* Shot in Argentina, a rare and expensive practice for a studio whose "location filming" often meant the mountains of California, *The Avengers* added rousing action and good acting to authentic scenery as it recounted the saga of bold Don Careless, who defends the early settlers of South America and wins the love of a patrician beauty. With John Carroll and Fernando Lamas to carry the action, it remained for Adele to sustain the romance; to make of love a quest as exciting as rescue. Winningly photographed in period costumes, she revealed the incontestable fact that a pretty girl had become a beautiful woman. Her spun-gold hair, riotous over her shoulders, coiled into intricate braids, or drawn in Roman fashion behind her head; her enormous eyes, alternating between aristocratic hauteur and womanly submission; a voice that, even commanding, retained the essence of femininity: thus did she rivet attention and give to the picture the quality of a folk tale for adults. The man who won the love of such a woman must seem a latter-day Robin Hood, and the woman herself a rarer Marion than she of Sherwood Forest. Herbert Yates, always the businessman, filmed a foreign version for showing in Mexico and Latin America, and the bilingual Adele articulated as sweetly in Spanish as English and won a large following south of the border.

Forrest Tucker.

The other two pictures of 1950, *Rock Island Trail* and *California Passage,* were expert escapist films, as good as all but the best of Wayne's own westerns for Republic. No one demanded the subtleties of *Angel in Exile.* It was more than enough that Forrest Tucker, who had been groomed for stardom in movies with Wayne (and has endured to this day, recently appearing in Max "Jethro" Baer's production, *The Fighting McCullouchs),* made a redoubtable hero, and that Miss Mara, in addition to making a star of her leading man, departed from those triple stereotypes of the Old West, the enduring wife, the prim schoolmarm, or the kind-hearted hooker, and performed with a spirit that matched her beauty, whether she was smudged with dirt and climbing the face of a cliff, or soft in laces and velvet and pliant for love.

Forrest Tucker wrote to me of Miss Mara (March 3, 1975):

> I have been asked to perform a most enjoyable task—to tell you my memories of working with Adele Mara.
>
> First—it was never work. It was joy. Adele is a LADY in capital letters and seemed to bring out the best in all of us. Cast and crew alike used our "company coming to dinner" manners.
>
> I haven't seen Adele in almost twenty years but I think of her every time I see velvet. Adele is made of velvet. Her eyes are a very soft brown velvet—her skin is ivory velvet—her mouth is pink velvet—her hair blows like silk, shines like satin but feels like velvet. Her laugh is absolute velvet.
>
> I can't really tell you anything personal about this charming lady because she always stayed about twenty yards from me. I don't think she likes the odor of tobacco or whiskey, which is what I smell like, so the only time I ever got close to her was when playing a scene.
>
> Those brief times bring happy memories because I like ladies and velvet.

Unhappily, strong performances and velutinous beauty could no longer assure her of stardom at Republic, a small studio stalked by television. The new industry, quiescent during the war, had staked a particular claim on the studio's first domain, the fast-moving action tale, western or eastern, rugged with heroes and docile with heroines. Furthermore, Republic's own giant, John Wayne, was soon to depart to bigger studios, and Miss Ralston's pictures, which Yates continued to film through 1958, failed to recover their cost without Wayne for insurance. In 1951, Adele was given a single picture, *The Sea Hornet,* the story of divers and dames in misadventures as dull as its leading man, Rod Cameron. The one original touch was Adele's name: Suntan. She had played such parts in her early days at Republic. Never an actress to repeat the past, she left the studio at the end of her seven-year contract, together with Dale Evans and Roy Rogers, to look for work appropriate to her skills.

But the lacklustre fifties were not a propitious era for high-powered women stars. The star system in general, for men as well as women, had begun its long decline. Glamour was leaving the screen; Hollywood, once a "garden of fantasies," was now compared to a factory. The flourishing careers of a few all-American favorites like Marilyn Monroe and Doris Day led both audiences and critics to overlook the portent in the decline of such immortals as Bette Davis, Olivia DeHavilland, Greer Garson, Myrna Loy, and Joan Crawford.

In eight years Adele made five pictures, only one of them appropriate to a star. In the inoffensive but mediocre *Count the Hours* (1953), she supported McDonald Carey and Theresa Wright, a ranch hand and his pregnant wife mistaken for murderers. *The Black Whip* (1956) is a cactus among westerns with two redeeming blooms, Adele and Angie Dickinson. *Back from Eternity* (1956) is an updated but inferior version of Lucille Ball's *Five Came Back* (1939), the fale of a plane crash in a jungle peopled by head-hunting Indians. *The Curse of the Faceless Man* (1958) is a horror movie in its horrendous misuse of a fine actress. Only her final film, *The Big Circus* (1959), shows her to advantage in an early spectacle produced by Irwin Allen, who recently capsized an ocean liner *(The Poseidon Adventure)* and set fire to a skyscraper *(The Towering Inferno).* Notwithstanding a modest budget, the superior script engages a large cast, Victor Mature, Rhonda Fleming, Red Buttons, Vincent Price, Peter Lorre, Gilbert Roland, Steve Allen, Adele Mara, and assorted trained animals in familiar but uncloying subplots subordinated to the major concern of saving the circus from its creditors and its rival. Miss Mara, an ageless thirty-six, plays an aerialist married to Gilbert Roland. Nicknamed "Mama Colinos" because she mothers the rest of the cast, she anticipates both Shelley Winters and Stella Stevens in *The Poseidon Adventure,* and Jennifer Jones in *The Towering Inferno.* Invariably Allen's most sympathetic women die a violent death.*

During the sixties she made occasional guest appearances on television and received the tribute

---

*Adele dies in a train wreck; Stella falls into burning oil; Shelley suffers a heart attack; and Jennifer tumbles out of a shaken elevator. Joan Fontaine, unsympathetic but understandable in *Voyage to the Bottom of the Sea,* is eaten by sharks.

of a profile in *TV Guide,* but her reign at Republic was so completely forgotten that Warren B. Meyers dared to list her among the "Tough Tomatoes" in *Who Is That: The Late Late Viewer's Guide to the Old Old Movie Players* (1967). Doubtless he remembered the gun molls and other schemers and forgot the cowgirls and collegians she had played at Columbia and then at Republic before she became a star. Surely he had forgotten her actual stardom. At least he could write: "Your prissy maiden aunt very likely clucked her disapproval, but in her secret heart she probably loved these tough tomatoes too, for one could always see the heart of gold, and the glint of good humor that lay just below the 'hard,' wise exterior." Furthermore, the picture he paints of Adele is a sparkling Sonja Henie, in furs and hood, looking readier for a sleigh ride than a seduction. In short, if Adele is a tough tomato, then every man should cultivate a garden.

No one need ask, "Whatever happened to Adele Mara?" Married to the distinguished television producer Roy Huggins, who won an Emmy for "Maverick" in 1958 and is currently producing the popular "Rockford Files," she emerged in 1973 to co-star with James Farentino in the short-lived detective series, "Cool Million." If the scriptwriters had allowed her to leave her switchboard and participate in the action, the series, badly in need of a strong, continuing woman's role, might have conquered the lethal Nielsons, with Adele and James anticipating the success of Angie Dickinson and Earl Holliman in "Police Woman." Nevertheless, Adele's telephone conversations were the highlights of the program. Looking half her age, she displayed both style and beauty, as well as a trait that can best be described as a twinkle, a sly way of saying to time, "Do your worst. You can't hurt me!"

What is a star?
Adele Mara.

# Epilogue

In 1946 the movie industry grossed the largest sum in its history, and Republic, profiting from its cheapest serial to its glossiest western, shared in the windfall.

In 1948 Milton Berle began his eight-year reign as Mr. Television.

In 1950 Herbert Yates founded Hollywood Television Service and started to rent his old pictures to the enemy; later, with rapidly falling grosses, he rented some of his own filming facilities to CBS.

In 1958, Republic released a mere fourteen pictures; in 1959, four. Even the tireless Yates had met his match; Jack the Giant-killer, had met the unkillable giant. He sold his entire studio to the Columbia Broadcasting System, and Republic, except for a foreign office still in existence, came to be known as CBS City, and its largest sound stage was adapted for telefilms. Still a wealthy man at seventy-eight, he retired with his wife and favorite actress to the seclusion that he had renounced in order to become the president of the only business in which he had failed.

Yates was a victim of his own early image. When he recognized the need for major productions, he was already and irrevocably branded as the western and serial king. Why should you buy a ticket to see Roy Rogers, the public began to ask? Television brought him into your house. Neighborhood theaters began to fail, and Republic pictures without John Wayne were exceptionally hard to sell to the metropolitan, one-feature houses. Yates needed stars—desperately—to lure, first the exhibitors, then the public.

True, the bankable names, the names so important that they could precede a title, were dwindling through the decade; still, there were rising stars, and many were women. Metro-Goldwyn-Mayer confronted the changing times with Debbie Reynolds and Elizabeth Taylor, and the fact that Liz had lured Eddie away from Debbie somehow endeared each of these disparate ladies to their fans (but wrecked the career of the shared male!). Twentieth-Century Fox employed and exploited that red-haired cyclone, Susan Hayward, and a lady of love and laughter, Marilyn Monroe. Universal launched a talent program and, unsuccessful with starlets like Mari Blanchard and Lori Nelson, planned increasingly important roles for Doris Day, a singing star when she entered the movies, and in 1959 with *Pillow Talk,* she began her enormously profitable series with Rock Hudson, in which the loss of virginity seemed more important than losing the Holy Grail. Audrey Hepburn, the only star whom the mammary-fetish fifties could forgive for her lack of breasts, enchanted Paramount—and the nation—with *Roman Holiday.* At Columbia Rita Hayworth kept her crown until Harry Cohn had groomed a replacement in Kim Novak.

But Republic's record with women, poor at the start, was inconsistent even when Yates had begun to look for talent behind a pretty face. Had he recognized the potential of Ann Rutherford, Carole Landis, Jennifer Jones in the early days— had he locked his mistress-wife in her private skating rink—had he found superior vehicles for his own contract player, Adele Mara, briefly a star because of talent, beauty, endurance, and damnably hard work—in short, a single woman star might have saved his studio (or John Wayne, if fear of working with Vera had not impelled him into the arms of Lana Turner and Sophia Loren—at other studios). After all, it was a teenaged girl, Deanna Durbin, who had rescued Universal in the late thirties.

Regrets, however, are fruitless. They cannot resurrect; they can only reproach. And, in a sense, Republic still survives. Early television (and much of the present) owes more to Republic than to any other studio. Quick, competent work on a limited budget was the secret of Republic's first successes; the secret, too, of many made-for-TV movies; westerns ("Gunsmoke" and "Bonanza"); detective shows ("Perry Mason" and "Mannix"); cornball comedies ("The Beverly Hillbillies" and "Petticoat Junction"). The daytime soap opera "Bright Promise" and the prime-time soap opera "Peyton Place" were, in effect, television serials for women, with every episode ending on a note of doubt, menace, despair to bait the casual watcher into a devotee, just as Republic serials had baited the boy or the man. An actor must know his lines; an actress must not expect meticulous photography from her most flattering angle (Yates had made one exception). Temperament was anathema; professionalism, the first necessity.

Such a survival in the victorious medium is not surprising. Republic technicians—cameramen—directors—producers—came to work for the networks even before the demise of Republic. Republic stars are still in abundance on the airwaves: Joan Blondell, Dale Evans, Martha Scott, Barbara Stanwyck, Eve Arden, Jeanette Nolan, Angie Dickinson, Ann Miller, Yvonne DeCarlo, to say nothing of men like Forrest Tucker, Rod Cameron, Roy Rogers—names without number. John Wayne guest-starred on "Maude" and stole the show from scene-stealing Beatrice Arthur. Susan Hayward, before her untimely death, hoped to star in her own series. Ann Miller, dancing atop a soup can, gave to the medium one of its best commercials. Myrna Loy is active in films as well as television.

Herbert Yates, the businessman, would have congratulated his old employees for finding work on the major networks (or looking eternally young in reruns of his old movies). But Yates, the dreamer, would have exulted that his personal dream, expanded through the years, has become a part of our cinematic heritage. Look at them, Republic's leading ladies—silent at first, shy, pretty, fragile: Ann Rutherford—yes, she will make a splendid sweetheart for Andy Hardy. Jennifer Jones—flashing a tentative smile. Then the women with spirit: Claire Trevor—the hard-talking whore—others disdain her but Wayne knows her hidden heart. Susan Hayward—even in black and white she seems to scintillate! And talk about fires: Yvonne DeCarlo, the Flame of the Islands and the Magic Fire! Maureen O'Hara, fiery of temper as well as hair! Adele Mara—the angel in exile—celestial vision, earthly longings. Ilona Massey—Hungarian style in the rude, rough West. Joan Crawford in *Johnny Guitar*: did ever a glamorous lady talk so tough—and yield so tenderly?

Look at them in the secret cave of the mind. Look at them with their men; finally *equal* to men.

The door to the cave is closed upon more than gold.

But memory is the abracadabra.

*She walks in beauty like the night . . . .*

# Appendix

An article that appeared (first serial rights only) in the *Tyrrean Chronicles* and discusses Adele Mara and Adele Jergens in their fantasy films.

### Let Down Your Golden Hair
### By Thomas Burnett Swann

Adele Mara was not of our workaday world; she belonged in a fairy tale: Rapunzel, billowing golden hair; Goldilocks, a maiden instead of a girl; Cinderella, ascending the steps of her coach. Adele, the actress, departed along with magic from the movies, leaving, however, that buried crock of gold, the rarity of her roles.

Gold comes in many colors, many values—silvery-white as foam in a burst of sun or rich as the bands on the back of a bumble bee; it is always, however, valuable, sometimes invaluable. Adele in her fifty-eight films (1941-1959) has left us many colors, and none more fine than her work in four fantasies for Republic Pictures. Alchemists's gold, what else? She is the priceless element from the alembic of a fabled alchemist, he who magicked the good into the best.

So extravagant a metaphor is not inaccurate. She worked for a small company, the so-called "Western-studio," on Hollywood's Poverty Row, not the Metro-Goldwyn-Mayer of Garbo and Crawford, nor even Universal, the home of the Wolf Man and Frankenstein, the Invisible Man and Maria Montez in assorted Arabian nights. Her fantasies for Republic—*The Vampire's Ghost* (1945), *The Catman of Paris* (1946), *Angel in Exile (The Blue Lady)* (1948), and *The Avengers* (1950), were little pictures befitting the size of Republic. They did not star John Wayne; they did not boast the splendors of Technicolor, Demille-like producers or name directors (except for Allan Dwan). Still, they seemed to have felt the alchemist's touch, and Adele was their incontrovertible gold.

*The Vampire's Ghost* was an inexpensive thriller, meant for the lower half of a double bill. The vampire's "African village" was built on Republic's lot, and the terror was only terrible to the young. Economy, not a vampire, was the curse of the film; mediocrity, the result: except for Adele as Lisa, the leading lady. She acted when "actors" around her read their lines; her voice was as sweet as the wind in a baobob tree; and when she danced she seemed to walk on the wind. Shakespeare might have called her a female Ariel. A modern poet, a dreamer of dreams born out of his due time, remembered her when he wrote:

> "I go," said the wind
> "To a yonder-land
> Where the dragon feeds
> From a Dryad's hand
> And the Centaur blows on a silver horn
> To call the unicorn."

*The Catman of Paris,* a costlier picture in every respect, starred Lenore Aubert, the Yugoslavian beauty, one of those foreign exotics whom Republic's President Yates engaged with increasing frequency in the forties and early fifties . . . . Vera

Hruba Ralston (Czechoslovakian, but alas, exotic only to Yates. She squinted); Ilona Massey, Viola Essen, Yvonne DeCarlo.... Miss Aubert was given the choice scenes, the finest costumes, the flattering camera angles in this chic, nineteenth century thriller, and indeed she pleased the eye and acted with style. But Adele in the second lead was more of everything: the greater beauty, the better actress, the stronger presence. The nominal leading lady joined Anna Sten and Sigrid Gurie and the legion of foreign actresses whom Americans refused to accept in major roles.

By 1948 Adele had worked at Republic for more than four years and filmed twenty-seven pictures. Yates, however, had yet to proclaim her a star. The choice women's roles he reserved for his mistress, Vera Hruba Ralston, or Judy Canova, the "hillbilly queen," or actresses borrowed from other and bigger studios (Claire Trevor, Joan Blondell, Susan Hayward).

Until 1948 and *The Blue Lady.*

The picture could easily have been a routine melodrama. Its male lead, John Carroll, had never escaped the tall, swaggering shadow of that more famous John, "Duke" Wayne, to whom he had lost the affections of Anna Lee in *The Flying Tigers.* Its director Allan Dwan was considered an aging and unreliable talent, who, it seemed, had forgotten the art combined with craft which he had brought to *Heidi, Suez,* and *The Three Musketeers;* and the fact that he had signed with minor Republic was taken to indicate that he was not in demand at Metro-Goldwyn-Mayer and the other major studios where he had once directed Tyrone Power, Loretta Young, and Shirley Temple.

During production the wistful and evocative title, *The Blue Lady,* was unaccountably replaced by *Angel in Exile;* the picture, little advertised, was shown in neighborhood, not metropolitan, houses; the *New York Times* ignored its release, and reviews in smaller papers were few and brief. But Yates, if slow, was never dense; he belatedly recognized another star on his lot and cast her with John Wayne in *The Sands of Iwo Jima.* * She had become her own alchemist.

Every true star is unique; to describe Adele Mara in terms of other actresses is pointless and demeaning. For it was her differences which made her a star. Say that Adele in her third Republic fantasy and Jennifer Jones in *Portrait of Jennie* and *Song of Bernadette* were magic-makers; say that both of them seemed to be earthbound against their will and destitute for a celestial haven, a lost and

*Republic's most profitable picture, directed by the "rejuvenated" Allan Dwan!

unearthly love; say and be silent, for they differ more than they meet.

*Angel in Exile* is not a melodrama; its violence is balanced by Adele's performance and her commensurate beauty. It is Adele who gives to the seemingly straightforward plot of a hardened thief reformed by a Mexican girl those intimations, those eloquent silences, which are the hallmark of almost every classic. Perhaps Adele is only the gentle peasant whom she appears; perhaps in truth she is an exiled angel, dimly remembering but resigned to remain on earth for a purpose she does not understand. "Perhaps" is the theme which helps to etherealize the mundane plot. The certainty is her beauty. The certainty is her performance, the great wondering eyes, the shy, tentative gestures, the voice which is "Greensleeves" sung to the notes of a lyre.

*The Avengers* (1950) is not in the strictest sense a fantasy; physical laws are not suspended; no supernal beings descend from heaven or ascend from Hell. Nevertheless, like *The Mark of Zorro* or *The Prisoner of Zenda,* like the old English folk tale of Robin Hood and Marion, it gives a feeling of purest fantasy. The place? A mythical country "somewhere in South America." The time? "When the early Spanish settlers were battling renegades." The characters? 1. Don Careless, a mysterious avenger, a patrician Robin Hood, who hides in the wilderness, assumes disguise to mix with his enemies, and defends the weak and the poor against the rich and the strong. 2. A lady whose face is out of a Botticelli, Spanish by name but strangely flaxen of hair, who helps Don Careless to help the weak and meets his love with the ardor of Sherwood's Marion.

Adele herself is the ultimate dream. She beguiles, bewitches, transcends; she epitomizes the fairy-tale princess with the golden hair (gold from the loom of Rumplestiltskin?). Her movies have moved from the overt fantasy of a vampire and a catman, to the probable fantasy of an angel descending to earth, to the spirit of fantasy in *The Avengers.* Ironically, it is her last and least overtly fantastic picture in which she is most a being of fantasy; in which she is one with Cinderella and Rapunzel, Goldilocks and the Sleeping Beauty.

Adele left Republic in 1951, filmed a ludicrous horror picture for United Artists in 1958, *Curse of the Faceless Man,* and enjoyed a quiet but distinguished television career as a guest star during the sixties. In 1973 she reappeared with James Farentino in the short-lived series, *Cool Million.* It was a detective caper, not a fantasy, and its only wonder lay in Adele. Those who remembered her from her Republic days were not surprised that she scintillated in a minor role. But she was fifty-one, and they looked in vain for signs of age, a wrinkled brow or a double chin. Like Rider Haggard's She, Adele had outwitted time. But then, in a fairy tale, it is only step-mothers (crafty) and witches (wicked) and godmothers (good, if you heed their advice) who are withered and gray. Rapunzel, Let down your golden hair. The world is dark and we have need of you.

## Aphrodite, Earthbound
### By
### Thomas Burnett Swann

Adele Jergens flourished in fantasy films, but she did not belong to a fairy tale. Her rightful home was Olympus, with Zeus (leering at her) and Hera (glaring at him) and the other nine Immortals, gathered to sup ambrosia and plan the affairs of men, both martial and amatory; for she was an incarnation of Aphrodite, the divine courtesan, adored by the women of ancient Greece, including the plain little wives who sat at the loom and envied their livelier sisters in the houses of pleasure or the groves of delight.

Adele might incarnate Aphrodite, the goddess of love; but bound for the moment to earth, she must utilize mundane means to become a star. A Powers model at seventeen, she became a singer and dancer in nightclubs and Broadway musicals and caught the eye of a Hollywood talent scout who saw her replace an ailing Gypsy Rose Lee (*Star and Garter*) and reveal a talent to match her Olympian looks. Harry Cohn of Columbia groomed her for stardom in microscopic roles and presented her to the public in *A Thousand and One Nights* (1945) as the least likely and most delectable Moorish princess ever to tantalize a prince. Cohn was having problems with his biggest star, Rita Hayworth, her frequent marriages and inevitable divorces, her retirements, salary demands, and disappearances.

To present Adele as a star in such a film was a fearful risk, since Universal, his chief competitor, had enthroned Maria Montez in Arabian epics. Miss Montez, so flamboyant that she did not need to act, was duskily red of hair and sweetly sinful of smile; and, prompted by Universal executives, producers had surrounded her with an entourage of dashing, adoring males—Jon Hall, who had weathered a hurricane with Dorothy Lamour; Turhan Bey, his almond eyes as teasing as his name; and young Sabu, abruptly famous from his lead in *The Jungle Book*. To the public at large an Arabian night without Maria was only meant for sleep.

Cohn must compete and compel; he must add a

night to the famous thousand and one, and enrapture his audience as Sheherazade had enraptured her restless caliph; otherwise, box-office execution.

He assembled a heterogeneous but high-powered cast; he set Adele like a perfect yellow diamond in a tiara of pearls, both black and white: Cornel Wilde, Columbia's handsomest male; Phil Silvers, a popular comic of Broadway and films; Evelyn Keyes, Scarlett's sister in *Gone with the Wind*; and assorted nubile maidens and murderous rogues. And he wisely supplied his players with a superior script; a script with a difference.

Instead of the vivid but humorless films of Universal, he demanded humor as well as spectacle: intrigue and battles, yes, and even Rex Ingram as a King Kong kind of a genie, who clutches Wilde in his hand as Kong had clutched his enemies and his ever-screaming love; but from time to time some quiet or hilarious fun—not camp, that vague, overused, and yet to be coined term; nor satire, farce, or parody; in a phrase, serious action lightened with comedy. Cornel Wilde must handle a sword as if he were dueling Fairbanks, father or son; Phil Silvers, an Easter egg atop a burnoose, must prove that wisecracks could also be weapons; Evelyn Keyes, when Barbara Eden was still a child and people who dreamed of Jeannie thought of a song, must play a female genie who befriended Wilde and promised to reunite him with his beloved but craftily plotted to get him into her lamp.

But the real surprise of the picture was Adele. Previously glimpsed on the screen in one serial and two features, she proved an apotheosis both to Wilde and the public. Arabic princesses, in keeping with their lineage, were generally played by black-haired women (June Duprez) or red-haired women (Maria Montez). Adele was a champagne blonde.

This tall, aureate woman might have been one of the famous Fox blondes—Faye or Grable or Haver or, later, Monroe—who had sinuated into the wrong film. But she looked such an Aphrodite, and she played the role of the Princess Armina with such disarming mischief and merriment as to quickly suspend disbelief and convince the movie-goer that Moorish maidens were fair instead of dark. When soldier of fortune Wilde removes her veil, the revelation surpasses the expectation, the facial striptease is far more seductive than total nudity.

The picture enthralled both critics and audiences. Wilde was acknowledged by *Time* as Hollywood's latest idol; Silvers climbed toward his highest fame as television's Sergeant Bilko; Evelyn

Keyes was handed the feminine lead in Columbia's lucrative hit, *The Jolson Story.* It was Adele, however, who received the greatest acclaim. Servicemen hailed her as the "princess of pulchritude." She received a breathless profile in *Collier's,* "Standing Room Only on a Coral Island," to say nothing of pictures (leggy) and articles (lusty) in papers and movie magazines. Cohn's publicity machine had proclaimed her a star; those who had seen her thundered a *yes* in italics.

But Rita Hayworth recognized the threat and quickly returned to the fold, amenable, even compliant. Cohn had spent a fortune to make her a star in extravagant musicals. It was just such films in which the Broadway-trained Adele could display her Venusian gifts. Rita made promises: She would limit her marriages, lessen salary demands, accept repetitious but proven scripts. Cohn rewarded her with the role of the goddess Terpsichore in *Down to Earth;* Adele was reduced to her naughty rival, dancing a single dance in garish undress.

Thus did Adele begin a decade of lesser parts in big pictures and leading parts in little pictures. Though denied her rightful stardom by the economies of a small studio and the whims of its dictatorial boss, she performed with unfailing skill and came to be known as Columbia's sexiest sinner. A moll or a murderess? A prostitute? A high-handed actress or a low-minded mistress? Send for Adele! Thanks to Cohn, a comely, competent dancer whose songs were dubbed and whose acting was adequate, held her position against a woman who sang her own songs, outstepped Terpsichore, and surpassed a serviceman's most seductive dream.

But Adele was a trouper as well as a temptress. In her first major role, she had graced an elaborate epic; in her last, made for Republic, not Columbia, she endured a low-budget "science fiction" story, *The Beginning of the End,** which was so preposterous and unscientific that it should have been called a bad fantasy. Adele was twenty-eight when she filmed *A Thousand and One Nights* (though

*Sometimes confused with a totally different picture, *The Beginning of the End,* starring Robert Walker, one-time husband of Jennifer Jones.

announced as twenty-four), forty in *The Beginning of the End.* She had played a princess of Baghdad; now she played a stripper, one of the few survivors of an atomic holocaust which has mutated most of her friends into grasshoppers more immense and voracious than tigers, and with an inclination for human flesh. Adele did not survive to the end of the picture; she provided a savory dinner for the mutants, among them co-star Lori Nelson's former love (notably less lovable with antennae and wings). One of the last pictures filmed by failing Republic, *The Beginning of the End* was both a prophetic title and a predictable box-office failure, even in double bookings.

Adele, however, had not lost her gold. She made a triumph of forty. Furthermore, unlike her listless companions, Peter Graves, Peggie Castle, and the love-lorn Miss Nelson, she acted as if she were toiling for that present-day tyrant of genius, Sam Peckinpah, who elicits great performances from good performers. To cheer her timorous friends, when the grasshoppers trap them in a deserted house, she enacts an imaginary strip without removing so much as a shoe or a glove and gives the illusion of a nude Canova Venus. She teases and tantalizes, she reaffirms that nudity in the imagination can be more erotic than in the flesh; and she brings to her role the pathos of a generous-hearted woman who shares her only gift—but what a gift!—to hearten her friends. Middle-age, crude black and white photography, apathetic co-stars, a hackneyed plot, a background of gross inaccuracies: Nevertheless, gold remains gold, and Adele glitters as flawlessly as in *A Thousand and One Nights.* Given a choice, any sensible man would have chosen Lori and not Adele for the grasshopper feast. But then, nobody really believed in those ridiculous insects . . . .

Adele and Adele: the fairy tale princess and the Grecian goddess; neither, thanks to their studio bosses, a major star in the annals of Hollywood. But those who saw them in their infrequent fantasies have placed them side by side, whatever their differences, in the sky of the imagination.

*Sunset and evening star . . . .* no, two stars, the brightest of the golds.

# Annotated Bibliography

Barbour, Alan. *John Wayne*. New York: 1974. A good but limited study of Wayne's more famous films; a chronological list of films to match the text.

Behlmer, Rudy, ed. *Memo from David Selznick*. Selznick, the great producer, revealed in his own letters, telegrams, and memos; a unique autobiography that reveals an extraordinary man, and, indirectly, the extraordinary woman he loved, Jennifer Jones.

Bogdanovich, Peter. *Allan Dwan: The Last Pioneer*. New York: 1971. An extended interview between a young, rising producer and an old, remembered producer. Several inaccuracies in the Introduction.

Carpos, George. *The John Wayne Story*. New York: 1972. A breezy account of Wayne's life and work; best on the early films.

Cawkwell, Tim, and Smith, John A. *The World Encyclopedia of the Film*. New York: 1972. Ignore the assertion that this is "the most comprehensive film encyclopedia available in any language." Good, but frustratingly less than the title claims.

Farnett, Gene. *Starring John Wayne*. Satellite Beach: undated. A book of black-and-white still shots from Wayne's most representative pictures dating back to 1930, with accompanying notes. A collector's item.

____.*Hollywood's Poverty Row:. 1930-1950*. Satellite Beach: 1973. A fine account of Hollywood's lesser studios. Accurate and informative, with many rare photographs from the author's own collection.

Fredrik, Nathalie, and Douglas, Auriel. *History of the Academy Award Winners*. New York: 1974. The title suits the text but does not indicate that this is one of the most handsomely produced paperbacks on the market, with the photographs, small of necessity, selected with care and reproduced with clarity.

French, Philip. *The Movie Moguls*. Chicago: 1969. A good treatment of producers, directors, and company executives, with helpful information about Herbert Yates.

Freulich, Roman, and Abramson, Joan. *Forty Years in Hollywood*. New York: 1971. The chapters on Republic, Universal, and other studios are good, but the photographs by Freulich are exceptional: Even Vera Ralston becomes a beauty!

Gelman, Barbara, ed. *Photoplay Treasury*. New York: 1973. A worthy compendium from the best movie magazine, from 1917 to the present.

Griffith, Richard. *The Movie Stars*. New York: 1970. Superior writing, poor arrangement of topics.

Halliwell, Leslie. *The Filmgoer's Companion*. New York: 1971. Imaginative entries on all aspects of filmmaking—actors, producers, directors, subjects, terms, etc. A jolly companion, indeed. Take it to bed with you.

Hanley, Loretta et. al. *TV Feature Film Source Book, Part I*. New York: 1972. The most complete listing of old films and their stars, with brief plot summaries and an occasional review. Invaluable.

Harmon, Tom, and Glut, Donald F. *The Great Movie Serials*. New York: 1972. Fun.

Haskell, Molly. *From Reverence to Rape*. New York: 1974.

A feminist history of movie actresses which leaves the impression that a woman would almost as soon be raped as revered. Read it as a conversation piece.

*International Motion Picture Almanac*. New York: 1973. Thorough if dull. Dip, don't browse.

Kobal, John. *Gods and Goddesses of the Screen*. New York: 1973. Graceful in text, becoming in photographs. A unified history of the American film.

Lamparski, Richard. *Whatever Became of . . . ?*. New York: 1967. The first of five well-researched and nostalgic compilations of yesterday's famous names.

_____. *Whatever Became of . . . ? (Fifth Series)*. New York: 1974. Sprightly reading about old favorites from every profession, emphasizing show business. Superior articles on Jane Frazee and Gail Storm. Beware of a slight tendency to select the sensational fact above the significant fact. A case in point: Adele Jergens, whose legs receive more attention than her talent.

Levin, Martin, ed. *Hollywood and the Great Fan Magazines*. New York: 1970. A testament to the literary excellence of the old movie magazines: for example, the biography of Ann Dvorak.

Maltin, Leonard, ed. *TV Movies*. New York: 1974. Mr. Maltin and his associates somehow manage to make several thousand plot summaries as engaging as their pithy assessments. Many notable omissions, however.

McCarthy, Todd, and Flynn, Charles, eds. *Kings of the B's*. New York: 1975. A history of the B-movie in Hollywood. Emphasis on directors and companies, not stars. Excellent text, poor arrangement.

McClure, Arthur F., and Jones, Ken D. *Star Quality*. South Brunswick and New York: A. S. Barnes and Co., 1975. A treasure of photographs.

Meyers, Warren B. *Who Is That? The Late Late Viewer's Guide to the Old Old Movie Players*. New York: 1967. Fascinating photographs and crisp comments, oddly arranged.

Michael, Paul, ed. *Movie Greats: A Pictorial Encyclopedia*. New York: 1969. Separate entries for motion picture players, directors, and producers of the sound era, each entry containing a complete list of credits and dates, and a photograph. Priceless.

Miller, Ann. *Miller's High Life*. New York: 1973. As zestful as its author.

Morella, Joe et. al. *Those Great Movie Ads*. New York: 1972. The history of filmdom revealed in its ads. Look and linger and *never* say that "Movies are getting better."

*New York Times Directory of the Film* (Introduction by Arthur Knight). New York: 1971. An index of actors and actresses, stars or supporting players, from 1913 to the present, with a list of the films they have made. Look under "Mala" and you will find that Republic's one-time serial queen made five features films, alternating between Polynesians and Indians. Also, almost two thousand photographs. Indispensible.

Ramer, Jean. *Duke: The Real Story of John Wayne*. New York: 1973. A tiny part of the story. By-pass this one for the better biographies of a great star.

Rosen, Marjorie. *Popcorn Venus*. New York: 1974. A feminist history of movie actresses. Enjoy the good writing, beware of the biases.

Sarris, Andrew. *The American Cinema*. New York: 1968. There is no better critic on today's movie scene, and here he maintains the excellence of his individual reviews in *The Village Voice*.

Scheuer, Steven, ed. *Movies on TV*. New York: 1974. A fine companion volume to leonard Maltin's *TV Movies*. Even together, however, the two volumes are less complete than *TV Feature Film Source Book*.

Schipman, David. *The Great Movie Stars: The International Years*. A useful account of the major movie stars, but sometimes inexplicably harsh and even cruel. Of Susan Hayward: " . . . if she's at her best in *I'll Cry Tomorrow* (she won an acting award at Cannes for it) she still isn't very good."

*Variety: 69th Anniversary Edition*. (January 8, 1975). An excellent overview of all the artistic media, with *Variety's* annual chart of the all-time top-grossing films.

Weiss, Ken, and Goodgold, Ed. *To Be Continued*. New York: 1972. The most thorough of the several recent books about movie serials. Plot summaries accompanied by still shots. Read, look, and remember.

Zolotow, Maurice. *Shooting Star: A Biography of John Wayne*. New York: 1974. The definitive life of Wayne, with careful attention to his films. Well-researched, well-written, well-edited. Buy it.

# Index